Playscripts for Primary Schools

QUESTIONS
PUBLISHING

Playscripts for Primary Schools

A resource pack of scripts for adaptation in the classroom

By Suzanne Brown

QUESTIONS
PUBLISHING

THE QUESTIONS PUBLISHING COMPANY LTD

BIRMINGHAM

2001

The Questions Publishing Company Ltd
27 Frederick St, Birmingham B1 3HH

First published in 2001

ISBN: 1-84190-040-0

Cover design by Arlene Adams
Printed in the UK

Contents

Introduction – using the plays

The plays

Purpose and procedure – why bother?

So at last, after what seems like months of work, with one hour of hall time, the children are ready, the adults are seated and the show begins. Chances are several of the props fall to pieces, a lead character has called off sick at the last minute and Mr and Mrs Smith want to know why Harold only had four lines when he had ten last year. It is at this point that we question: Why?

We may have asked this before, of course, while trying to negotiate hall time or combining the demands of rehearsal with SATs preparation. But it never seems quite so acute a concern as when the result of your efforts is made public property. With the pressures of the current Key Stage 2 curriculum, teachers are increasingly required to justify the time spent on even the most deserving of activities.

The fact that our cries of "never again" have usually changed to "well, next year I think we should …" by the end of the performance is evidence of the durable benefits of putting on a production with children. Despite that hard work and occasional lack of appreciation from individuals, generally the school play is well received, satisfying, and one of those occasions that remain with children and adults as lifetime motifs.

This pack of plays aims to make the task of presenting the play easier. But it also represents more than that. It is born out of the belief that plays need not just be an end of year or Christmas production. I believe that working together with variously sized groups of children is a valuable curricular activity which can suit many other purposes as well as the more traditional production.

Many of the plays in this pack are intended for use at other times of the year:

○ for mother's day;
○ to reinforce and introduce aspects of history topics;
○ for preparing children for transfer to secondary school;
○ as one way of opening up discussion of the meaning of equal opportunities.

They are, variously, intended to be much more than a 'production'. At a time when we may feel the need to justify every hour spent, this material will help to provide a legislative excuse for our indulgence.

I believe that working together on a script, or an outline of a script, can be an extraordinary 'bonding' process for a group. The cooperative demands of adaptation, prompting and preparing in anticipation of a presentation, often highlight the best (and worst) of our capabilities.

Jack Zipes, in *Creative Storytelling*, refers specifically to the value of dramatisation and production as a means of creating communities within schools. Although his work is based in the United States, there is no doubt that many of the concerns he expresses about the lack of opportunity for children to engage and interact with the negative messages they receive via the media, are also applicable in the United Kingdom.

The work of Betty Rosen, in *And None of it was Nonsense* and *Shapers and Polishers*, is further evidence of the importance of interaction and the power of storytelling and dramatisation. Encouraging interactions will help our children to take control of written and oral forms, feeling themselves empowered. Scripts and storytelling provide a link between oracy and literacy, which is essentially valuable to the English curriculum.

Dramatisation is a powerful tool, which is often an accessible means of expression for children who are less 'traditionally academic'. Quite often, those who find reading and writing difficult are adept at expressing themselves vocally, and find the opportunities to 'perform' in an acceptable context a powerful way to raise their self-esteem.

All the plays in this pack have been tried and tested. They have been used with Key Stage 2 children in an inner city school with great success. The productions have not always been 'polished', alterations have been made, and a variety of problems addressed. Without a doubt, those benefiting most have been the children who do not always achieve success in other areas of the curriculum. I could relate countless anecdotes involving the satisfaction that these children have had in hearing their efforts applauded. Parents, who normally would not enter school, have turned up to watch and to congratulate in a previously unheard-of fashion.

Children who have spasmodic attendance records have arrived at school repeatedly in order 'not to let the side down', and their achievements have been recorded in photographs and videos for all to see, re-live and evaluate. I am sure that these moments, no matter what difficulties they may face in the future, have given them something positive to take from school. As their teacher, it convinces me each time that it really is worth it.

The introduction to this pack of plays does acknowledge the demands of the National Curriculum and attempts to provide teachers with a *raison d'être* that will satisfy the curriculum planners. However, its basic premise is that the cross-curricular benefits of these productions far outweigh the contribution to programmes of study. The chart 'Creativity in curriculum planning' details how using these plays will support National Curriculum coverage in a way that engages children's attention and brings the curriculum to life.

The chart 'Script summary' gives a brief overview of the plays included, although each play also has a summarised introduction that enables a quick flick through for a suitable script. A central premise of these scripts is that improvisation by children, adaptation to context, and owning the production, should be central to the process. In some cases, the scripts are simply a framework of ideas for linking children's own unscripted plays. In others, there is a more detailed script framework with opportunities for amendment and adaptation. The leavers' concerts tend to be more formal and less open to adaptation. The real finale.

Finally, 'Applications – making it special' provides a guide to using the scripts. It anticipates that the suggestions here are a starting point and acknowledges that the creative potential of individual groups of children and their teachers will enable a whole range of alternative productions and scripts to follow.

Creativity in curriculum planning

How to bring the National Curriculum to life

The following chart provides a cross-reference from each play to the National Curriculum. There are, of course, many cross-curricular benefits as well. Every production involves the children in invaluable skills of:

- cooperation;
- reliance upon one another's contributions;
- working towards a shared goal;
- involvement of parents and other adults in the school community;
- opportunities for raising self-esteem;
- experiencing approbation and recognition;
- problem solving;
- evaluation;
- patience.

At times when schools are often experiencing difficulties with unmotivated children and their families, opportunities to develop the skills mentioned here can be life-savers. I believe behavioural difficulties often emerge from the frustration resulting from an inability to master the basic skills and benefit from the National Curriculum. By enabling children with reading and writing difficulties to express themselves and receive recognition for their oral skills, I have witnessed behaviour being moderated, and previously castigated members of the school community suddenly finding themselves valued and approved of. Although I do not suggest that this reverses the frustration and solves their lack of skills acquisition, I do believe it gives them a step from which to begin to tackle some of the problems that may have caused their negative behaviour. It is a starting point.

Other curricular skills are evident and appropriate for every play and need not be repeatedly identified. In particular:

- collection of props and opportunities for associated art work;
- inventive adaptation of props using technology skills;
- speaking and listening skills;
- reading aloud skills;
- use of standard and non-standard English;
- importance of, and interpretation of, punctuation;
- reading and writing scripts.

The National Literacy Strategy includes many references to the use of scripts as part of the text level work to be covered (Table 1).

Plays and play scripts are included in the range of work for Term One in each of the four junior school years. Using these play scripts will provide a basis from which to discuss conventions of scriptwriting and the changes needed, and special considerations involved in adapting familiar stories to play format.

For example, the play *The golden goose* could be used as a springboard for adapting other fairy stories and well-known myths and legends. This particular play also lends itself to discussing how stories can be placed in different contexts and more modern settings.

Table 1

Year 3 Term 1	To read, prepare and present play scripts.
Year 4 Term 1	To prepare, read and perform play scripts; compare organisation of scripts with stories – how are settings indicated, story lines made clear? To chart the build-up of a play scene, e.g. how scenes start, how dialogue is expressed, and how scenes are concluded. To write play scripts, e.g. using known stories as a basis.
Year 5	To understand dramatic conventions including the conventions of scripting (e.g. stage directions, asides); how character can be communicated in word and gesture; how tension can be built up through pace, silences and delivery. Write own play scripts, applying conventions learned from reading; include production notes.
Year 6	To prepare a short section of story as a script, e.g. using stage directions and location or setting.

Table 2 Play titles and links with the curriculum

Play title	Page	Curriculum area	Curriculum link
Last day at school	2	Personal & social education	Review of primary school years – liaison and discussion regarding secondary school
Lazy Bear and Hard-working Hare	7	Personal & social education	Stories with a moral; Planting, nurturing and harvesting
It's not fair	15	Equal Opportunities; History	Issues concerning representation of women in resources, playground games, advertising and media; History – Key Stage 1 programme of study – lives of different kinds of famous men and women, including personalities drawn from British history
Who needs parents?	26	Social & moral education	Role of parents – importance and value of 'carers'
War journeys	33	History	Study unit 3b: Britain since 1930
I'm Henry VIII – honestly!	39	History	Lists Henry VIII's wives and reflects upon the style of life which might have led to his large frame
The *Sinking Rat*	45	Design & technology; Social & moral education; Media studies	Design & technology – Key Stage 2 programme of study – designing and making through the creation of props, scenery and costumes; Roles of the media
The battle of Bean and Sprout	65	Design & technology; careers education	Design & technology programmes of study – Key Stage 2 – designing and making through the creation of props, scenery and costumes; Morals and values in business; Present and past shopping habits

Table 2 Play titles and links with the curriculum *continued*

Play title	Page	Curriculum area	Curriculum link
The disciples go shopping	87	Religious education; Literacy;	The stories Jesus told, the role of the disciples; Transferring stories to new contexts – updated versions through different media; The effect of the market economy on shopping choices – the demise of the town centres
The golden goose	93	Citizenship – consumers markets	Fairy tales as a genre; Stories with morals – the moral of this tale
Mystic Joseph	98	Literacy; Social & moral education	The story of Joseph – different presentations of the story; Egypt and the effect of famine
So you think you're going home tonight?	104	Religious education; Geography	Evacuation and going into hiding – Anne Frank; The effect of separation and working together as an isolated group
Promise you won't look	109	History; Citizenship Literacy; Religious Education	Stories with a common theme of a warning being ignored; Myths, legends and religious stories from different cultures using the theme of the warning ignored

Table 3 Play titles, purpose and summary

Play title	Page	Time	Cast	Purpose	Summary
Last day at school	2	15 min	15 speaking parts – potential for more	Leavers' assembly – Year 6	Rachel reminisces about her primary school experience. Through a series of short sketches she reflects on past school days and speculates about secondary school.
Lazy Bear and Hard-working Hare	7	20 min	14 parts	A play with a moral about doing things for yourself – a good harvest assembly	Mr Bear always relies upon others doing the hard work for him. After a series of tricks by Mr Hare, he learns it is best to do the work for himself. As crops are grown and harvested throughout the play, it links in well with harvest celebrations.
It's not fair	15	20 min	41 speaking parts – potential for more	Equal opportunities	A 'hit squad' of children tries to sort out a range of problems involving unfair treatment and inequality. Light-hearted play with a serious message.
Who needs parents?	26	15 min	33 approx.	Mother's day/assembly on the role of parents	A group of parents go to a party and leave their children to fend for themselves. Groups of children begin to realise just how important their parents are. Light-hearted but important message.
War journeys	33	20 min	28 speaking parts – potential for 60 parts	Play to support a 'Britain since 1930s' topic	Sketches based just before and during the war on the theme of 'journeys'. It includes evacuees, the land army, air-raid shelters, Jarrow march.
I'm Henry VIII – honestly!	39	10 min	19 speaking parts – 2 non-speaking and potential for more	An assembly for a class or year who are covering the Tudors	King Henry makes an appearance on stage. The children are surprised that he doesn't look as fat as he does in their history books. Henry tries to explain how he got to be that way – large banquets and his wives get the blame.

Table 3 Play titles, purpose and summary *continued*

Play title	Page	Time	Cast	Purpose	Summary
The *Sinking Rat*	45	45 min	60 parts	Leavers' concert	An old-fashioned sailing ship acts as a gathering point for a kidnapped boy and a stowaway. Light-hearted entertainment with custard pies included.
The battle of Bean and Sprout	65	45 min	60 parts 19 speaking parts	Leavers' concert	A supermarket sets up in competition with a local greengrocers. A light-hearted entertainment with custard pies and other pantomime traditions included.
The disciples go shopping	87	20 min	9 major parts 10 smaller parts	Harvest assembly	The disciples have to find some bread and fish to feed the five thousand. How will they do it? Contemporary setting.
The golden goose	93	15 – 20 min	10 main parts plus a chorus	Assembly – stories with a moral	The traditional story in script form with some contemporary additions. Originally performed with Year 4 children.
Mystic Joseph	98	10 min	13 parts with potential to extend	Harvest assembly	A contemporary version of part of the traditional story of Joseph. A good lead-in to exploration of the rest of the story and other versions using different media.
So you think you're going home tonight?	104	10 min	12 parts	Assembly with the theme of evacuation – living in hiding	A class of children is told that they are unable to return home. This is a short play during which the children come to realise what the implications of this might be in a light-hearted fashion.
Promise you won't look	109	10 min		Assembly with the theme of ignoring advice and temptation	This play is made up of a selection of short sketches using different stories all involving individuals who cannot resist the temptation of taking a peek or ignoring the advice they've been given. all with interesting consequences!

Applications – making it special

If you are looking for a play to perform in its entirety, then some of these scripts will be ideal. *The Sinking Rat* and *The battle of Bean and Sprout* are ready for copying, rehearsing and presenting. Others need customising to your own school and circumstances.

Children particularly appreciate customised plays that include familiar names, current trends, and language. Even the more detailed scripts allow some room for incorporating localised references to teachers, schools, rules and key characteristics of the individuals associated with the productions. The plays can be grouped according to two categories:

② scripts with opportunities for improvisations to be incorporated;
② scripts where names and some details might be changed to personalise them.

Category 1	Category 2
Last day at school War journeys Who needs parents? So you think you're going home tonight? It's not fair	The *Sinking Rat* The battle of Bean and Sprout The disciples go shopping The golden goose Mystic Joseph Promise you won't look Lazy Bear and Hard-working Hare I'm Henry VIII – honestly!

Some suggestions for where adaptations might take place are incorporated in the script. Emboldened names and sections will need changing or adapting to suit your own context.

Some of the scripts may encourage discussion about important issues within the school. *It's not fair* raises many issues to do with equal access in school which could form the basis for discussion. This might result in alterations to the scripts and/or sketches being incorporated. The next chart highlights cross-curricular themes that may arise from using particular scripts.

Table 4 Cross-curricular questions

Play title	
Last day at school	What do we mean by temptation? What are you, or have you been, tempted to do that you know you shouldn't? Which of these situations would you find most difficult to resist? How could the individuals have avoided the temptation?
Lazy Bear and Hard-working Hare	What is the moral behind the story? Can you think of any other stories with the same message? What do you think life would be like in the bear household in ten years time? What do we mean by being 'lazy'? What is the difference between being lazy and relaxing? Does anyone ever describe you as being lazy? What for? What other stories do you know of that have a message about how we should behave?
It's not fair	What do we mean by a gang? What groups do you belong to? How could we categorise people in this class? Why do we categorise people?
Who needs parents?	What are you looking forward to about being an adult? What do you think are the disadvantages of being an adult? How could you help out more at home? What responsibilities do you have at home or at school? What responsibilities did your parents have when they were younger? How is life different for children nowadays from when your parents were children?
War journeys	Why did the Jarrow march take place? What would you be prepared to march for? What ways do people have of protesting now? Have you stayed away from home? What would you miss if you were evacuated? What possessions would you take with you if you were evacuated? What are the differences between city and country life? Would you rather live in the town or the country?
I'm Henry VIII – honestly!	What would it have been like to meet Henry VIII? Do you think you would have liked him? What other aspects of his life might have led to his eventual ill health and appearance? Which of his wives do you feel most sorry for? How do you think kings and queens have changed since then? Would you have like to be a king or queen in Tudor times? Would you like to be a king or queen in Britain now?

Table 4 Cross-curricular questions *continued*

Play title	
The *Sinking Rat*	Do people listen to you? Have you ever thought about running away? what problems would you face running away from home? Were there pirates? Are there pirates now? In what ways are the characters in the play stereotypes? Which newspapers do you read? Are journalists justified in behaving as they do? How would you advertise a job in school?
The battle of Bean and Sprout	Where do you go shopping? Do you prefer large or small shops? What stereotypes are in the play? Which pantomime traditions can you spot? what pantomimes have you been to see? Why have supermarkets become more popular? What do you think shops will be like in the future? How could we make shopping easier? How do shops differ in different areas or countries? What rules and regulations do we have that traders have to take notice of? Are these important?
The disciples go shopping	What are the strengths or weaknesses of modern shopping centres? How have they changed and is it for the better or worse? What might this play suggest to us about modern life? If the disciples were living now, what other problems might they encounter? How tolerant are we of people who are different?
The golden goose	Why is a sense of humour important? Why did the youngest son end up with the golden goose? Which stories with similar messages are you familiar with? Does it always work out that the kindest is rewarded? What other rewards might there be for being kind?
Mystic Joseph	Do you think that dreams have meanings? What do you think about the way in which Pharaoh decided who to release from prison? Did Joseph earn his release?
So you think you're going home tonight?	What would you miss most about not being able to go home? How would you feel? What might the problems be if you were to spend a lot of time with just the people from your class? How might your problems change the longer you were isolated? Which of the characters do you feel most sorry for? Is there anyone you don't feel sorry for? Why? How would you feel if you were told you couldn't go home this evening? You can choose five items to take with you on a desert island – what would you choose? Have you ever been homesick – how did it feel?
Promise you won't look	Can you keep a secret? What secrets shouldn't you keep? Do you have a secret hiding place? Are there places in your house where you are not allowed to look?

The plays

Last day at school

Purpose: Originally written for a leavers' assembly, this play could be used to instigate discussion with Year 6 children or as a stand-alone performance for a wider audience.

Summary: Rachel reminisces about her primary school experience. Through a series of short sketches, incidents from her school days are presented. These include reflections on the first day at school, receiving reports, and conclude with speculation about secondary school.

Approximate running time: 15 minutes in its current form but additional sketches could be added.

Number of speaking parts: Rachel and her teacher take the two largest parts with an additional 13 speaking parts.

Total number of potential parts: More children could be involved by increasing the number of visiting secondary school children and incorporating more sketches.

Prop requirements: This play can be performed without any props, although some paper to represent letters, the report and a bin, might be useful visual aids.

Level of child intervention/adaptation: There is much potential for additional sketches to be inserted. Children could be responsible for suggesting ideas for these themselves, e.g. school dinners, school trips, the nativity.

Other comments on presentation: This is a very simple play to rehearse and perform, and can be prepared quite quickly. It can act as a stimulus for much useful discussion about the children's worries about moving schools. Children could even prepare their own memories montage for performance, or as part of a written assignment.

Last day at school

Rachel and Miss Brown stand centre stage and introduce scenes from Rachel's past school experiences

Miss Brown	Well, Rachel, this is your last day at school. I hope you enjoy your secondary school as much as being here.
Rachel	So do I!
Miss Brown	You have enjoyed being here, haven't you?
Rachel	It's certainly been an experience.

Rachel and Miss Brown freeze and Rachel turns to the audience

Rachel	Most of the time is has been a good one – experience that is – though there have been times when . . . well, let me show you. Now, to start with there was that very first day . . .

Enter child with parent, child reluctantly digging in her heels; exit Rachel and Miss Brown

Child	I don't like it!
Parent	You haven't been yet.
Child	I don't like it!
Parent	Look, all the other children are going in.
Child	I don't want to!
Parent	Look, if you're a good girl, you can have a packet of crisps at home time.
Child	I still don't like it.
Parent	A packet of crisps and a drink then.
Child	I still don't like it.
Parent	A packet of crisps, a drink, a comic and a **troll** [substitute any toy currently in fashion]?
Child	I like it!

Exit child and parent, enter Rachel

Rachel	*(to the audience)* And so began my years at **Park School** [substitute own school name], although I wasn't aware of quite how long they'd keep me there.

Exit Rachel; enter parent – child rushes on and hugs him or her

Parent	Did you have a good day?
Child	Great. I got covered in sand and I played outside all day.
Parent	I am pleased you enjoyed it.
Child	Can I have my crisps, drink, comic and troll now?
Parent	I suppose so. But don't think you're going to have these treats every day.
Child	Every day? What? You mean I have to go there again?

Exit parent and child, enter Rachel

Rachel	*(to the audience)* So that was the day I first realised that life

would never quite be the same again. But if school was a mystery to me, it certainly was to my parents. They could never keep up with what was happening.

Rachel moves to side of stage; enter parent, child runs out to him or her and dumps her bag on him or her

Child	Can we stop at the shop, Mum [or Dad]?
Parent	*(sarcastic)* Hello Mum, how are you Mum?
Child	Can we?
Parent	Have you got your reading book?
Child	These are for you. *(gives parent a whole pile of paper)*
Parent	What's all this?
Child	Some letters for you.
Parent	But some of these are from last year! 'Dear Parent, welcome to your child's class **1996** [or whatever year] . . . ' Why didn't you bring it home before?
Child	I forgot.
Parent	This one is for last year's open evening – 'Come and discuss your child's progress'. I didn't get much chance did I?
Child	They got inside Jenny's drawer.
Parent	They shouldn't have been in anybody's drawer, should they? Let alone Jenny's.
Child	I don't know what happened – I just forget sometimes, that's all.
Parent	It might as well go in the bin now. *(goes to the bin and stuffs all the letters in)*
Child	Don't do that!

Parent pushes them all down in the bin

Child (cont)	*(shakes head)* You shouldn't have done that.
Parent	Give me one good reason why not.
Child	There's something . . . I think it's a pink one . . . or maybe a blue one . . . *(starts rummaging around in the bin)*
Parent	What are you on about?
Child	There's one you've got to sign for tomorrow!
Parent	*(wails, head in hands in despair)*

Parent and child exit

Rachel	My parents tried really hard, bless 'em. They read all the letters – those I took home, that is. They went on sponsored walks. They helped with the **Autumn Fayre** [or any other school event]. They even tried to discuss what I'd actually been doing in school. Really, they should have known better . . .

Child sat watching television, parent enters the room

Parent	It says that we should ask you about what you're doing in topic at the moment.
Child	*(still absorbed by the TV)* Oh.
Parent	So, what have you been doing today, love?
Child	This and that.
Parent	Did you do any maths?

Child	Might have . . . can't remember.
Parent	Did you do any writing?
Child	Yeah, I think so . . . perhaps.
Parent	Reading?
Child	Can't remember. Don't think so.
Parent	There must be something you remember doing!
Child	*(jumps up, suddenly inspired)* I know. Yes! Yes, we did do something!
Parent	*(very enthusiastic now)* What? What?
Child	Oh . . . um . . . sorry. It's gone again. *(sits back down to watch TV)*
Parent	*(wails, head in hands in frustration)*

Exit parent and child, enter Miss Brown

Miss Brown	Here you are, Rachel. Don't forget this. *(hands over report)*
Rachel	Oh no! Thanks Miss Brown. Very kind of you. *(turns to the audience)* My report. How I hated report day. Although maybe not to start with. I can remember there were some years . . .

Enter parent clapping Rachel on the back; exit Miss Brown

Parent	Well done! Super! 'Tries hard', 'Great effort', 'Always kind', 'Very polite', 'Good standard all round', 'Keep it up'. *(exits)*
Rachel	*(to the audience)* Trouble was, I didn't. Keep it up that is. I got a little tired of the same comments and went for a slightly different version . . .

Enter parent throwing arms up in despair

Parent	Rachel, how could you? After all we've done for you! Look at this. I quote, 'Rachel has not tried her hardest this term . . . Rachel is capable of much better work . . . Rachel does not always manage to concentrate . . . Rachel sometimes has difficulty maintaining her concentration . . .' The shame. The humiliation. It's that Jenny, isn't it? She's always been a bad influence.
Rachel	If you say so.
Parent	I knew you should have sat near the front. I said right at the start . . .
Rachel	If you say so.
Parent	If only . . .
Rachel	Yes?
Parent	If only . . . if only . . . Oh, I give up!
Rachel	Got it in one!

Parent exits, shaking head

Rachel	But now it's all over. The good and the bad. I think I'll keep my reports . . . all of them. Just to remind me. And next term?

Enter Miss Brown

Miss Brown	You're not worried, Rachel . . . are you? The stories haven't put you off, have they? Bullying in the playground, heads down

	the toilets, that cruel maths teacher?
Rachel	Me? No! Don't be silly. I know they're only meant to scare us.
Miss Brown	Here come some of last year's leavers. why not ask them?

Exit Miss Brown; enter leavers

Leaver 1	*(shakes head)* Secondary school? Don't ask!
Leaver 2	You wouldn't want to know.
Leaver 3	You arrive there on your first day . . .
Leaver 4	And your uniform looks all new.
Leaver 5	And you don't know where you're going.
Leaver 6	And everyone points you in the wrong direction.
All	And . . . and . . . and . . .
Rachel	Yes, yes, yes?
All	We're the biggest load of fibbers to ever leave this school . . .

All run off laughing except for Leaver 6

Leaver 6	Honest Rachel. It's not easy starting a new school. But everyone feels the same, or has felt the same, and after the first few days you feel like you've been there forever. This place . . . *(looks around)* . . . just seems really small now. Tell you what, first day there, I'll help show you round.
Rachel	Will you? Brilliant! *(turns to the audience)* Well, bye everybody. Bye Miss Brown. Enjoy the rest of your time here. I'll look forward to seeing you again . . . if you don't see me first.

Lazy Bear and Hard-working Hare

Purpose: This is a useful play for supporting a harvest celebration. Its message is that in order to reap rewards, you must be prepared to sow something first. The main character, Mr Bear, tries his best to avoid putting any effort into obtaining food. Mr Hare, on the other hand, is able to outwit him to the point where Mr Bear is forced to acknowledge the need to do something for himself. The use of animal characters to convey a message can be linked with a whole variety of fables and folk tales.

Summary: Mr Bear's family are tired of finding nothing in the fridge. Mr Bear owns land but is not prepared to work it. Mr Hare suggests a deal in which he works on Bear's land and then splits the crops at harvest time. The first time this happens, Mr Bear asks for the top of the crops as his share. He discovers that Mr Hare has planted carrots. When Mr Bear asks for the bottoms, the crop is lettuce. And, finally, when he opts for both tops and bottoms, he is still not successful as Hare has planted sweetcorn. In the end, Mr Bear concedes defeat and agrees that, perhaps, he needs to work the land for himself.

Approximate running time: Between 15 and 20 minutes.

Number of speaking parts: There are 14 parts with four major speaking parts.

Total number of potential parts: Additional children could be included by extending the hare and bear families and introducing other animals when Bear is trying to rid himself of the unwanted roots and shoots.

Prop requirements: Older children are unlikely to want to dress themselves in costume for this but might be persuaded to wear some kind of token. The play does benefit from 'dynamite' at the end, as this is difficult to portray otherwise.

Level of child intervention/adaptation: The characters could really be any animal or even human. Children could choose different crops or add more tricks for Hare of their own. Comparisons might be made with cartoons such as *Roadrunner*, where an animal is constantly outwitted. They could try creating their own plays and dramas based upon this concept. Colin McNaughton's *Boo* and Pat Hutchins' *Rosie's Walk* display the same characteristics. Children could seek out other picture book examples and try writing scripts of their own.

Emphasis can be placed upon the 'feuding neighbours' dimension. The two households could be interviewed on a talk show or could be seen plotting against one another in other contexts.

Other comments on presentation: The success of this play depends upon the acting strengths of the two main characters. A strong couple of personalities will result in an amusing conflict that they will find difficult to live down.

Lazy Bear and Hard-working Hare

Bear is lying on stage, snoring, Mrs Bear walks on with a rattle

Mrs Bear	I'll get him up if it's the last thing I do! *(starts to shake the rattle)*
Mr Bear	*(jumps out of his skin and runs backwards and forwards)* What's happened? *(sees Mrs Bear)* Oh, it's you! Well thanks a lot. I was just having a lovely dream about tomato soup and chips.
Mrs Bear	Bears don't eat tomato soup and chips! Come to think about it, if you don't do some work soon on the farm, we won't be eating anything, let alone tomato soup and chips.
Mr Bear	Will you stop fussing! Can't a bear get a bit of sleep around here without listening to you? Nag, nag, nag. All the time. There's plenty of food in the cupboard.
Mrs Bear	Plenty of food in the cupboard? You must be joking! Have you looked in our cupboards recently?

Baby Bear and teenage Bear come running in

Bear 1	I'm starving, Mum. What's for tea?
Mrs Bear	There's plenty of food in the cupboard. Help yourself.
Bear 1	*(looks in cupboard)* It's empty, except for this rotten tomato and I'm not eating that! *(storms out)*
Bear 2	What a day I've had. Those hares really get on my nerves, working all the time. They've always done their homework.
Mrs Bear	And what about your homework?
Bear 2	I can't do my homework till I've had something to eat. I'm famished. What's for tea?
Mrs Bear	It's in the cupboard.
Bear 2	IN the cupboard? There's nothing in the cupboard but a mouldy old tomato, and I'm not eating that!
Mr Bear	All right, all right. I get the message. But if you think I'm doing any work for a living you'd better think again.
Mrs Bear	Right, you lazy, good-for-nothing, poor excuse for a grizzly bear. Just you get this spade between those good-for-nothing paws, take yourself out of this house and start digging!
Mr Bear	Or else?
Mrs Bear	Or else!
Mr Bear	You'll do what?
Mrs Bear	I'll . . . I'll . . . *(bursts into tears)*
Mr Bear	All right, all right. You think I'm not up to much, don't you? You think I'm lazy and I do nothing but sleep! I'll show you – I'll show you all!

Stage clears, Mr Bear exits and returns with the spade

Mr Bear	Digging indeed. Just because I own lots of land that my father gave me, she thinks I have to do something with it! Over my furry muzzle. I'll just have to find someone else to do the dirty work. But who?

Enter spider man

Mr Bear	Ah! Anansi spider man could you do a spot of digging for me?
Anansi	I'd love to help out, Bear. Really I would. But as you know I'm all legs and no arms, so I can't do any digging for you! *(exits)*
Mr Bear	*(shouting after him)* Fine friend you are!

Enter fox

Mr Bear	Ah! Here's Brer Fox. Could you do a spot of digging for me?
Fox	Goodness me, and get dirty brown soil all muddled up with my lovely red coat? I think not, Bear. I think not. *(exits)*
Mr Bear	Fine friend you are!

Enter tiger

Mr Bear	Ah! Here's Tiger. It wouldn't take him long, I bet! Here, Tiger. Fancy a bit of digging?
Tiger	*(roars)* Only if it's digging my claws into your hairy fat flesh!
Mr Bear	*(jumps out of skin)* Help! Okay, I get the message. I'll . . . I'll let you off this time!
Tiger	*(roars)* I should think so, small fry! *(exits)*
Mr Bear	*(whispering)* Fine friend you are. *(louder)* Ah! Here come my neighbours, Mr and Mrs Hare.

Enter Mr and Mrs Hare

Mr Bear	*(to the audience)* Between you and me, they haven't got two pennies to rub together. Now, I know we haven't got a lot of spare cash, but it's all tied up in the land, you know. Just look at the state of them. Not an ounce of flesh on them. *(to Mr Hare)* Mr Hare! How nice to see you. If you're not too busy and fancy earning a penny or two, I've got a spot of digging to be done.
Mr Hare	It's funny you should mention that.
Mr Bear	It is?
Mr Hare	Because I was just going to suggest that you and me might be business partners.
Mr Bear	You were?
Mr Hare	Yes, I was.
Mr Bear	What kind of business partners?
Mrs Hare	We thought that, seeing as you've got some land but don't like digging . . .
Mr Hare	. . . and we like digging but haven't got any land . . .
Mrs Hare	. . . we could help each other out.
Mr Hare	And when the crops have grown, we'll split them down the middle, 50 – 50.
Mrs Hare	Half-and-half.
Mr Bear	Hang on a minute. Can this be real? You're telling me that all I have to do is let you dig my land and you'll give me half the crops without me lifting a paw?
Mr Hare	You don't even have to get out of bed to make the tea.
Mrs Hare	We'll do the lot!
Mr Bear	It's a done deal!
Mr/Mrs Hare	Right, sign here . . .
Mr Hare	Just one more thing. You'll need to decide whether you'd like

| | the top of the crops or the bottom. |
| Mr Bear | Top half or bottom half? I'll take the top. That's bound to be the best bit. |

Mr and Mrs Hare exit; Mr Bear returns home and prepares for bed

| Mr Bear | I'll set my alarm clock for the end of summer when the crops should be ready. Where's my teddy? *(hangs up sign 'Do not disturb – and that especially means you, little bears and Mrs Bear')* |

As Bear sleeps, the hare family come on to the stage digging, planting and reaping

The hares	Oh lazy bear you think you're cool
	But we will make you such a fool
	We'll dig this earth and plant the seed
	But it's not you we'll feed.

Hare 1	When you said you'd gladly share
	You didn't check, oh silly bear
	What food we'd plant, not form nor type
	But now the food is nearly ripe.

Hare 2	You'll smack your lips and love to taste
	But you will only get the waste
	For lazy bear your deal is dud
	The goodness lies below the mud.

Hare 3	You asked for tops, the choice was yours
	But you'll return with empty paws
	For as we harvest up these crops
	You'll find no carrot in the tops.

The hares run around Bear, ringing bells and shouting

Hares	Wakey wakey. Wakey wakey.
Mr Bear	*(snorts and jumps up)* What the . . . Oh, it's you lot. Is my half ready then?
Mr Hare	It sure is. Just look in the shed and you'll see all the tops waiting for you.
Mr Bear	Oh goody, goody. I'm so hungry.
Mrs Hare	Enjoy your meal *(giggles)*

Exit the hares

Mr Bear	Mrs Bear! I told you I'd sort out some food for us.
Mrs Bear	*(running on stage)* Well, about time too. Now where is it?
Mr Bear	Right over there, in the shed. Go on then, and take a look.
Mrs Bear	*(disappears behind the screen and comes back holding out a carrot top)* Right. So we've got lots of carrot tops. Where are the carrots though?
Mr Bear	Carrots? They planted carrots? The cheating scoundrels . . .
Mrs Bear	Well, it's not a sausage, is it?
Mr Bear	No, it's definitely not a sausage. And without its bottom, it's not a carrot.

The young bears come on

Bear 1	I am definitely not eating that!
Bear 2	Gross! Looks like you've done it again, Dad!
Mr Bear	Wait till I get my hands on that scrawny little hare!

The young bears and Mrs Bear disappear behind the screen and come out carrying suitcases.

Mr Bear	Where do you think you're going?
Mrs Bear	To my mum's. When the cupboard's full, let me know.

Exit Mrs Bear and young bears; Mr Bear walks around with a basket filled with carrot tops

Mr Bear	Maybe if I can't eat them, I can sell them to someone. There must be somebody out there who enjoys eating carrot leaves.

Enter rat

Mr Bear	Hey rat! You're not choosy. How about a nice cheese carrot top without the cheese?
Rat	Rotten meat and carcass droppings Grain and wheat and your mum's shopping There's lots of food I like to chew But carrot tops – they taste like pooh!

Exit rat; enter crocodile

Mr Bear	*(tastes a bit)* It doesn't taste that bad! Hey, crocodile! How about a nice fish pie with carrot tops but without the fish?
Crocodile	Wriggling frogs and silvery fish Make a very tasty dish Ripping flesh, swallow quick But carrot tops – they make me sick!

Exit crocodile

Mr Bear	That does it! He's really had it now. Hare! Where are you?

As Bear exits stage to walk around the back, the hare family enter and sit around a table, tucking into their meal; Bear comes around the other side of the stage to discover them

Mr Hare	Oh Bear! How nice of you to join us. What a shame we've just polished off the most delicious carrot soup and carrot cake.
Mrs Hare	If we'd known you were coming, we would have saved you some.

Mr Bear seethes, but struggles to get any words out

Mr Hare	What's the matter, Mr Bear? You don't look very well at all.
Hare 1	Dad, is there something stuck in his throat, do you think?

Mr Bear	Stuck in my throat? I wish there was something stuck in my throat. I wish there was carrot soup and carrot cake stuck in my throat. But no, all I've got in my throat is fresh air – or maybe it could be replaced by fresh hare . . . *(he starts to chase Hare around)*
Mr Hare	All right, all right. I can see why you're upset. Tell you what, I'll plant the crops again this year. We'll do all the digging, the sowing and the weeding, and this time . . .
Mr Bear	I'll have the bottoms and you can have the tops!
Mr/Mrs Hare	It's a done deal.

Mr Bear returns home and prepares for bed

Mr Bear	I'll set my alarm clock for the end of summer when the crops should be ready. Where's my cuddly polar bear? *(hangs up sign 'Do not disturb – and that especially means you, little bears and Mrs Bear', but crosses out the last bit)*

As Bear sleeps, the hare family come on to the stage digging, planting and reaping

The hares	Oh lazy bear you'll never learn Your tasty treats you'll have to earn Free lunches are too hard to find You've got to get off your behind.
Hare 1	You think the bottoms will taste sweeter We've got you sussed, oh hairy cheater Not carrots will the ground reveal But something further from a meal.
Hare 2	If you'd only use your brain You'd realise that you're tricked again We've left the carrot seed at home And lettuce is the crop we've sown.
Hare 3	Lovely lettuce, we can't wait Our mouths are watering at such a rate Juicy leaves and tender shoots But all you're getting are the roots.

The hares run around Bear, ringing bells and shouting

Hares	Wakey wakey. Wakey wakey.
Mr Bear	*(snorts and jumps up)* What the . . . Oh, it's you lot. Is my half ready then?
Mr Hare	It sure is. Just look in the shed and you'll see all the bottoms waiting for you.
Mr Bear	Oh goody, goody. I'm so hungry.

Exit the hares

Mr Bear	At last. I wonder what they planted this time. Carrots again? Or potatoes? I can't wait. *(passes behind the screen)* Hare! Hare! You thieving poor excuse for a rabbit! *(comes out at the other side of the screen, holding up just the roots.)* Lettuce roots! He planted lettuce and I've got all the roots. This means war.

	(brings out TNT, moves offstage and walks around to Hare's house and sets up the dynamite outside) Hare! That had better not be lettuce soup I can smell!
Mr Hare	*(not yet realising what Bear has planned)* Well, Mr Bear. Funny you should mention that. We've just finished a lovely bowl full of mouthwatering lettuce soup. How were the roots, Bear?
Mr Bear	Oh, just fine. And to thank you for your generosity, I've got a lovely little surprise waiting for you out here, Hare.
Mr Hare	*(starts to come to the door)* Oh, you shouldn't have bothered. My birthday's not till . . . *(sees the TNT)* . . . now Bear, just hang on a minute.
Mr Bear	Hang on a minute? I've been hanging on for two years, and all I've had from you are carrot tops and lettuce bottoms. Now it's jugged hare I'm going to be having for my tea. Say your prayers, Hare!
Mr Hare	Wait! I've got an idea!
Mr Bear	It had better be a good one.
Mr Hare	The problem is, you're not very good at making choices. When you chose tops, we just happened to plant carrots. When you chose bottoms, we just happened to plant lettuce. how about this time you have both the tops and the bottoms? Then you can't go wrong.
Mr Bear	This isn't another one of your tricks, is it Hare?
Mr Hare	As if I would . . .
Mr Bear	I suppose if I have both, I can't go wrong really, can I? Can I? *(Mr Bear asks someone from the audience what he should do. He agrees to let Hare have one more chance and exits from the stage with the dynamite.)*

Bear exits and hare family look worried

Mr Hare	That was close.
Hare 1	Dad! What do you mean, he can have both the tops and the bottoms? What are we going to eat then?
Mr Hare	Don't you worry. Just wait and see.

Hares exit and return ready to dig

Hare 1	Bear is going to shout and rant When he sees our current plant He thinks that he has really got them By asking for both top and bottom.
Hare 2	At first we were somewhat confused What was left to eat, we mused But Dad as ever solved the riddle There's tops and bottoms and also middle.
Hare 3	So when our bear collects his whack He'll want to put the whole lot back For now we'll share our latest fiddle All the sweetcorn's in the middle.
Hare 1	Hang on. I still don't understand!

Mrs Hare	Look. If we take off the roots, they're the bottoms, and the tassels, they're the top, what are we left with?
Hares	Yum, yum. We're left with the middle and that's our dinner!

Enter Bear

Mr Bear	Did I hear you mention dinner?
Mr Hare	You heard us mention 'our' dinner.
Mr Bear	Now wait a minute. Because this year I'm having tops and bottoms.
Hares	And we're having the middles!
Mr Bear	Middles? Nobody mentioned middles before. What plant has a middle?
Hares	*(holding up their sweetcorn)* This plant. And this is the middle and it's ours!
Mr Bear	*(jumps up and down in a rage on the spot)* That's it! That's it! If having tops doesn't work, and having bottoms doesn't work, and having tops and bottoms doesn't work, then . . . then . . .
Hares	Then?
Mr Bear	I'll just have to get off my lazy bottom and plant my own!
Hares	Yes!
Mr Hare	At last. You've got the idea. Nothing comes from nothing, Mr Bear.

Enter Mrs Bear

Mrs Bear	Did I hear right? Are you really going to get down to some work at last?
Mr Bear	Oh, Mrs Bear! Am I glad to see you? Yes. I promise. I've turned over a new leaf.
Mrs Bear	If that's the case, then you'll be needing this . . . *(goes off stage and comes back with a spade)* and this . . . *(goes off stage and returns with an apron)* You can start helping me around the house a bit, as well!
Mr Bear	Oh no! what have I let myself in for?

It's not fair

Purpose: A light-hearted look at some equal opportunities issues. Originally written for an 'equality' assembly, it can also form the starting point for discussion about equal opportunities in the classroom and in general.

Summary: A hit squad of children try to sort out a range of problems involving unfair treatment and inequality. There are four separate cases to solve, including a dispute over playing football, the ways in which toys are advertised, lack of women role models in non-fiction books and the ways we judge people by external difficulties.

Approximate running time: 20 minutes in its current form, although there is opportunity to add additional sketches and cases to solve.

Number of speaking parts: This is suitable for a class, or even two classes, to present. The children working on the sketches can do so relatively independently. Altogether there are 41 independent speaking parts, with the potential for at least another 10 or 15 more as part of a chorus.

Grouping arrangements: The four groups can rehearse on their own with the squad acting as the link group. This enables the majority of rehearsal time to go ahead independently.

Main characters: Frank is a major, lead character, and requires an individual who can time their appearances well. The other main parts are fairly equally divided.

Prop requirements: The performance will be enhanced by the squad being dressed in superhuman dress, e.g. capes. The toy advert sketch requires a doll and toy fire engine, and would benefit from the director being dressed in a suit, with a briefcase. In the women hero sketch, it would be an advantage if children could dress in costumes of the period. But it is not essential. The final sketch does require a number of woolly hats and fluffy scarves.

Level of child intervention/adaptation: Some of the sketches could be replaced by issues of particular concern to the individual school, e.g. the argument over playing football may have its more relevant equivalent. Different solutions to the conundrums could also be discussed and alternatives put forward in place of those suggested.

It's not fair

Enter the 'It's not fair squad', a gang of children dressed up as superhuman characters with masks and capes. They are ready to go out and spot incidents of injustice and sort it out. They appear regularly throughout the play to challenge people. Their leader is **Frank Fairbrother** *[or could be Fatima Fairsister]. They make their entrance by running around in front of the audience in search of something.*

On a signal from Frank, they all congregate around their leader

Frank	Well? Have you seen anything?
Squaddie 1	Lots of children!
Frank	I know that! I mean, is there anything that isn't fair going on out there?
Squaddie 2	What do you mean, Boss?
Frank	Oh for a team with brains! We're supposed to be the 'It's not fair squad', remember? We're supposed to go around looking for people who aren't treating each other fairly or equally.
Squad	Oh yeah, we remember! *(they jump up together and face their audience for the refrain that they repeat regularly throughout the play)*
	If you've got a problem
	If life's just not fair
	Dial this winning number *(holds up card with number)*
	And wham, bang, we'll be there! *(children turn to each other and clap hands while 'wham, banging')*
Frank	You've got it at last. Well, has anyone dialled you yet? Have you seen any action?

They all shake their heads

Frank	What a hopeless set of drivelling idiots.
	For goodness sake
	Stay awake
	There could be people's lives at stake
	You've got a job
	Now show you care
	By making sure that it's all fair!

The squad and Frank exit to the side of the stage, but always remain close to the action, ready to leap on at the appropriate moment

Enter group of girls

All	It's not fair!
Girl 1	Anyone would think they're David Beckham [or whoever else is topical] the lot of them.
Girl 2	*(imitating)* 'Out of my way!' 'It's my shot!' What a load of rubbish.
Girl 3	It's not even as though we want to join in their game. We just want some space.
Girl 4	Have you noticed what happens when they miss?

Girl 5	Yeah! They lose their tempers with each other and start to fight. *(imitates fighting)*
All	It's not fair!

They stand, leaning against each other looking fed up. Boys enter and walk past with their arms raised, swaying and singing. They don't look where they are going and trip over the first girl's foot

Boy 1	*(turns around angrily)* Who did that? *(turns to each girl in turn)* Was it you? Was it you? I'll . . . I'll . . . marmalise you!
Girl 1	I did it, actually.
Boy 1	What did you want to do that for?
Girl 1	Because I'm fed up of you showing off and taking up all our space.
Boy 1	Ah. Diddums.

Boys and girls stand back to back, arms folded

Boys	Who can't take the pace? Who'll have a little cry? They always have a problem And then won't tell you why.
Girls	You never, ever listen To what we have to say You all stay deaf to others We can't stop your play.
Boys	Ah, girls! *(heads in hands)*
Girls	Ah, boys! *(heads in hands)*
All	We don't understand What makes you tick All we really know Is you make us sick!
Girls	Ah, boys! *(hands around their own throats)*
Boys	Ah, girls! *(hands around their own throats)*

Enter the squad

Squad	If you've got a problem If life's just not fair Dial this winning number And wham, bang, we'll be there!
Frank	'Ello, 'ello, 'ello. What seems to be the problem here then?
All	*(point to each other)* They are!
Frank	Who is?
All	They are!
Frank	Now, putting two and two together, I see we have a little misunderstanding. *(walks around them, looking them up and down)* With my experienced eye, I see we seem to be a little confused.
Girls	He takes up all the space.
Boys	She doesn't know how to play.

Girls	He doesn't give me half a chance.
Boys	When we do you never stay.
Frank	Right, squad. We have a problem. Confer! *(squad go into a rugby scrum)*
Squad	*(mutter, mutter, mutter)*
Frank	Do you have an answer?
Squad	Yes we have an answer.
Frank	Is it a goody?
Squad	Yes it's a goody.
Frank	Right then, time to share.
Squaddie 3	*(holds up list of rules)* [these rules can be made to suit the school] Rule 1: Football area will be for girls only on Thursdays, and boys only on Fridays. Rule 2: For the rest of the week, any child may play football in that area. Rule 3: All children have an equal right to use the space.

Squad turn to each other and shake hands

Squad	Sorted.

Girls and boys turn to each other and shake hands

All	Sorted.

As girls and boys exit, the boys start to try and recruit some of the girls to their football teams; squad retreat to sidelines again

Enter a board of directors with briefcases

Director 1	So *(holds up a fire engine)*, this new toy. What shall we call it?
Director 2	Fireman Fred's Fantastic Fierce Fire Engine?
Director 3	Yeah! Let's make it sound really mean. How about Fierce, Flame-catching, Fire Quencher for Gladiators?
Director 4	The fire engine with bite.
Director 5	Now you're talking. What shall we put in the adverts? After all, it's coming up to Christmas. We want to sell as many as possible over the next few weeks.
Director 6	We'll have to have some boys pretending to put out a fire, won't we?

Enter boys – screech to a halt, making fire engine sounds – pretend to hose down a fire and follow subsequent instructions from the directors

Director 7	Then they could freeze and say something like, "Wouldn't it be better if we had a real fire engine?"
Director 3	Yeah. That sounds good. How do we get a real fire engine?
Director 5	We don't, silly. In comes Mum with our 'Fire Quencher for Gladiators' fire engine *(Mum enters and hands over the engine)* and it all ends happily with them saying it's the best Christmas present they've ever had.
Director 1	Right. Next toy. *(holds up a doll)* It burps, does little wee-wees and has a bottle. Any suggestions for a name?
Director 4	Just Real Judy?
Director 7	Tickle Toes Tracy?

Director 6	Lavender Laura?
Director 3	I like it. Brilliant! Lavender Laura. We'll sell them in their thousands.
Director 1	How shall we advertise Lavender Laura then?
Director 2	We'll need two girls of course.

Enter two girls who act out the instructions as the director describes them in the advert

Director 2	They're playing with their dolls but get fed up because their dolls don't really do anything. They start to moan about how they'd really like a real-life doll.
Director 3	How can we get them a real-life doll? They don't exist!
Director 5	Don't be silly. They don't get a real-life doll. Mummy buys them Lavender Laura. *(Mum enters and gives children Lavender Laura)* They're so happy because Lavender Laura burps and wee-wees that they have their best Christmas ever.
Directors	Ah.
Director 2	And even better, we make lots of money!
Directors	*(stand up and cheer)* Yeah!

Enter the squad

Squad	If you've got a problem If life's just not fair Dial this winning number And wham, bang, we'll be there!
Frank	Now then, now then . . . we can't have this!
Director 1	Can't have what?
Director 3	Do you want a fire engine too?
Frank	We most certainly do not!
Director 3	Well, Lavender Laura?
Squad	Be quiet!
Director 2	What seems to be the problem?
Frank	Your adverts are not fair.
Directors	*(look at each other confused)* Fair?
Director 1	They're not supposed to be fair. They're supposed to make us lots of money!
Frank	I'm sorry. But I'm going to take away your toys and your adverts *(starts to collect the toys from the amazed-looking children)*, until you've learned that your adverts should show how both girls and boys might like to play with a fire engine, and how both girls and boys might like to play with a doll.
Squaddie 6	And why shouldn't Dad give out some of the Christmas presents for a change?
Squad	*(nod in agreement)* Quite right too!
Director 1	So if we mix up our adverts a bit *(swaps some of the advert children around from one advert to another)*, is that any better?
Frank	Much better. By the way, I don't suppose I could keep one of these *(picks up a fire engine)* or perhaps one of these? *(picks up the doll; everyone looks at him strangely)* Not for me, you understand. For my brother's children. You know how it is …

Squad approach Frank, shake their heads, take the toys away from him and shake their heads

Squad	Sorted! *(dust off hands and exit to sidelines)*

Enter group of children with schoolbooks

Child 1	Research again!
Child 2	Well, I love it. It's great looking in books. *(they sit down together and start leafing through a pile of books)*
Child 3	Now, what have we to find? Stories about heroes for the heroes and villains assembly.
Child 4	Ah, look at this. **Winston Churchill** [heroes could be changed depending on current topics].
Child 5	Do you think David Beckham's a hero?
Child 6	I suppose so, in a way. He is certainly important to a lot of people.
Child 4	What about Tony Blair?
Child 3	Muhammed Ali?
Child 1	Do you notice anything?
Child 6	It's getting a bit cold in here?
Child 5	We could do with a few more books?
Child 1	No, I mean do you notice anything about these heroes?
Child 2	They've all got brown hair?
Child 3	He hasn't, he's bald!
Child 1	Don't you see? *(stands up angrily)* They're all men!
Child 2	Well, there can't have been any women heroes.

Children freeze as drums begin to beat, heralding the entry of a group of women with banners. Women march to the front and address the audience

Women	Votes for women! Votes for women!
	We want, we want votes for women!
	Votes for women! Votes for women!
	We want, we want votes for women!
Emmeline	*(steps out in front of the other women)*
	Mrs Pankhurst is my name
	I didn't think it fair
	Whenever time to vote was called
	Women were not there.
	Women could wash and clean and cook
	Women could mend your coat
	Women could do the servants' work
	But weren't allowed to vote.
Women	It wasn't fair!
Emmeline	We argued, chanted, made a fuss
	At last the right was won
	Now you vote but boy, oh boy
	It seems we haven't done.

> We look in books, they should be there *(picks up a book)*
> The famous artists with long hair
> The heroes in a skirt or dress
> Have been left out of books I guess.

Women	Before you think they don't exist Have we got news for you There's lots of women heroes here We bet you never knew.
Emmeline	Helen Keller! Come on down!

Helen Keller enters from among the women, does a twirl and bows to the audience

Woman 1	Helen Keller. 1880 to 1968. Blind and deaf but she still learned to talk, and she wrote books and gave lectures about her experiences.
Helen	What am I?
Women	A hero!

Helen Keller stands at the side of the stage and is joined by the other heroes as they are called on to the stage and introduced

Emmeline	Whina Cooper! Come on down!

Whina Cooper enters from among the women, does a twirl and bows to the audience

Woman 2	Whina Cooper. 1895 to 1994. A Maori woman who argued against white farmers taking Maori land in New Zealand.
Whina	What am I?
Women	A hero!
Emmeline	Arwa bint Asma! Come on down!

Arwa bint Asma enters from among the women, does a twirl and bows to the audience

Woman 3	Arwa bint Asma. 1052 to 1137. A Muslim queen who ruled fairly and well, in spite of difficult circumstances.
Arwa	What am I?
Women	A hero!
Emmeline	Anita Roddick! [heroes could be changed according to preferences]Come on down!

Anita Roddick enters from among the women, does a twirl and bows to the audience

Woman 4	Anita Roddick. Born 1943. Opened the Body Shop, selling creams and lotions made from natural products.
Anita	What am I?
Women	A hero!
Emmeline	Helen of Troy . . .!
Child 1	*(unfreezes and comes to the front of the stage from behind the women)* Excuse me, excuse me. *(turns to the women)* I get your point. And I'm really pleased to see so many women who were heroes. The trouble is *(slaps the book)* there is nothing in here about it. It's not fair!

Enter the squad

Squad	If you've got a problem If life's just not fair Dial this winning number And wham, bang, we'll be there!
Frank	Now then. What's happening here? A little assistance is needed I believe!
Child 1	We've been sent to do some research on heroes and can't find any information about women who were heroes. What shall we do?
Frank	Right, squad. We have a problem. Confer! *(squad go into a rugby scrum)*
Squad	*(mutter, mutter, mutter)*
Frank	Do you have an answer?
Squad	Yes we have an answer.
Frank	Is it a goody?
Squad	Yes it's a goody.
Frank	Well, what is it, team?

Squad come out of the scrum and hand out paper and pencils to all the children

Squaddie 1	There you go. Interview them for yourselves. And when you've finished, make sure you write it down so that other people can read all about it.
Squaddie 2	And can I recommend this book? 100 Greatest Women (Drayon's World, ISBN 1-85028-307).

Exit famous women

Squad	Sorted! *(shake dust off hands)*

Chanting noise can be heard in the background, the squad turn around to face it

Frank	Hang on. What's happening here?

Off stage, a gang who call themselves 'the woolly hats' are chanting

Woolly hats	Woolly hats! Woolly hats! We love We love Woolly hats!
Frank	What on Earth is that?

Five children come marching on, wearing woolly hats; they line up on stage and carry on marching

Woolly hats	Woolly hats! Woolly hats! We love We love Woolly hats!

Hat leader	Hold it! I can hear them coming. *(woolly hats cup their ears)*

Noise coming from off stage of a gang called 'the fluffy scarves', who are also chanting

Fluffy scarves	Fluffy scarves! Fluffy scarves! We love We love Fluffy scarves!
Hat 1	Let me at 'em, boss. *(others restrain him)* I'll show 'em which is best. Fluffy scarves indeed. Woolly hats are ten times better!

Enter the fluffy scarves gang marching; they line up opposite the woolly hats gang

Fluffy scarves	Fluffy scarves! Fluffy scarves! We love We love Fluffy scarves!

They stop marching when they see the woolly hats

Scarf leader	What are you doing here?
Hat leader	No. What are you doing here?
Scarf leader	I asked you first!
Hat leader	So?
Scarf leader	So?

The two gangs are now stood opposite each other, menacingly

Woolly hats	Woolly hats are the best You can wear them with a vest Cover up your ears and see Just how cosy hats can be!
Fluffy scarves	Fluffy scarves are the best Pull them tightly round your chest Under chins they'll keep you cosy Right up to your little nosy!
Woolly hats	Woolly hats we always win Throw those scarves into the bin.

Gangs approach each other, even more menacingly

Fluffy scarves	Woolly hats get them off They won't stop a nasty cough.

Squad intervene

Frank	What's going on here? Woolly hats? Fluffy scarves?
Hat leader	It's them! They've always had it in for us. Fluffy scarf wearers hate woolly hat wearers. That's the way it's always been and that's the way it always will be.

Scarf leader	And who can blame us? Just look at the state of you.
Scarf 1	You look ridiculous.
Hat 1	You look pathetic.
Scarf 2	You look diabolical.
Hat 2	One more word from you lot and I'll call in the anoraks.
Scarf 2	Oh yeah? Well, we'll call in the wellington boots!
Hat 3	If you don't stop, I'll tie all your scarves together.
Scarf 3	I'd just like to see you try!
Hat 3	Yeah?
Scarf 3	Yeah!
Hat 3	Yeah?
Scarf 3	Yeah!
Scarf 4	If you touch our scarves, I'll snip off all your pompoms.
Hat 4	You wouldn't dare!
Scarf 4	Yes I would.
Hat 4	Oh no you wouldn't.
Scarf 4	Pass me the scissors! *(a big pair of scissors are passed down the line from one fluffy scarf gang member to another)*
Frank	*(comes to centre stage)* Time to call in the squad. Right squad. Off with their hats! *(squad advances and pulls all the hats off)* Right squad, now off with their scarves. *(squad advances and pulls all the scarves off)*

Both groups look very confused without their scarves and hats

Frank	Can't you see how silly it is not liking somebody because of the way they look? Underneath, you're all the same!

Gang members all come forward and have a good look at each other. They pick up their scarves and hats and give them to one another and shake hands

Hat leader	Hey! I have to admit, this scarf feels really gorgeous!
Scarf leader	This is the most woolly hat I've ever worn. That scarf suits you. It matches your eyes.
Hat leader	That hat is just your colour as well. Do you think we should have a word with the anoraks and the wellington boots? I'm sure they could do with a swap as well.

All the gang members walk off together, hand in hand

Frank	You see. We're all the same underneath. Well team. You've done a good job in the end. We've sorted out some tricky problems. In fact, we've made the world a much fairer place.
Squaddie 1	There's only one problem left.
Frank	What's that?
Squaddie 1	How come you always get to be the leader?
Frank	Ah well, not everything can always be fair you know ...

Squad approaches Frank menacingly; Frank backs away

Frank	Now come on. Be reasonable. I'll start being fair tomorrow ...

Squad continue marching towards him

Frank   Well, this afternoon then!

Squad pick him up and carry him off

Frank   Help! It's not fair!
Squad   Oh yes it is!

All exit

Who needs parents?

Purpose: This play is meant to be presented for Mother's Day, or on a similar occasion to emphasise the important role of parents in our lives. Ideally, the parents' parts can be acted by the children's parents themselves, or alternatively the children take the roles.

Summary: A group of parents decide they have had enough of household chores and they are going to relive some of their youth by going to a club. Groups of children return home to discover the houses empty. There are four returning groups of children. The first group complain because there is no tea ready. The second group discover there is no-one home to take them to their different clubs and events. The third group are amazed to discover that the mess in the house is not caused, as they think, by burglars, but is how the parents left the house that morning. The final group are besieged by people demanding money, e.g. milkman, newspaper deliverer, etc. The parents return, after a less than successful evening, to discover that they have been missed.

Approximate running time: 15 to 20 minutes. Additional groups of children could be added to increase the number of children involved and the length of the play.

Number of speaking parts: This is a good play for the even distribution of parts. There are no major characters but 33 small speaking parts. For those not wishing to speak, there are opportunities for three non-speaking postal workers.

Prop requirements: The props required are minimal. A box of dressing up clothes is essential for the parents to get ready for their night out. The door to door traders might each carry a token of their job, e.g. a milk bottle, a newspaper, etc.

Level of child intervention/adaptation: Additional sketches could be added with children making suggestions for other ways in which they would miss their parents. Children might have other suggestions from their own experiences, e.g. different clubs they visit and need lifts for; their own favourite/least favourite foods, etc.

Who needs parents?

Two groups of parents enter; on opposite sides of the room they mime cleaning around the house – vacuuming, dusting, cleaning windows, etc

Group 1	Day in, day out Where can we be found?
Group 2	Working!
Group 1	Day in, day out Up to our ears in . . .
Group 2	Soap suds!
Group 1	Day in, day out Backwards and forwards
Group 2	Ironing!
Group 1&2	Is it all worth it? We really need to know It's sometimes tough To do enough And the boredom starts to show. We've time to think Stood at the sink Of how things used to be When we were out And having fun Instead of cooking tea.
Parent 1	*(flings down the duster and starts jumping on it)* No more dusting! No more scrubbing! I would rather go out clubbing To the night spots Disco dancing Chatting, drinking And romancing.
Parent 2	Well, why don't we?
Parent 3	What's stopping us?
Parent 4	They wouldn't even notice we'd gone.
Parent 5	But I've nothing to wear!
Parent 6	*(brings on a box of dressing up clothes)* You have now!

Parents dive into the box in a frenzy and quickly dress in all kinds of weird and wonderful ways – they mime admiring each other, shaking their heads, holding clothes up against each other, until there is a knock at the door

Driver	Your coach is ready

The rave is starting
All on board
We're departing!

Forget the mice
Forget the pumpkin
Rinse your hair
And pull your stomach in!

Parents line up in twos behind the coach driver and exit; enter a group of six children all carrying bags and school books

Children	Mum! Dad! We're home!
Child 1	I'm starving!
Child 2	I'm ravenous!
Child 3	Where's my tea?
Child 4	I hope it's not beans again.
Child 5	And if it's frozen pizza I will scream!
Child 1	Can you smell anything?
Children	No.
Child 2	Can you hear the sound of sizzling food?
Children	No.
Child 3	Can you hear the rattle of pots and pans?
Children	No
Child 4	Something's wrong.
Child 5	I think we should send out a search party.

Group of children start darting about, pretending to search under chairs, open doors; suddenly there's a knock on the door – all the children stop; a postman hands a letter to Child 6

Children	*(all gather around)* What's it say? What's it say?
Child 6	*(reads letter)* Dear all, I've decided to go away I'm sure you'll manage for just one day I'll be back quite soon I'm sure Don't forget to lock the door! Love Mum.
Child 1	But I'm hungry!
Child 2	I want her back!
Child 3	It's cold in here.
Child 4	And beans aren't so bad.
Child 5	Anyone fancy frozen pizza?

The group all sit down together looking fed up as another group of children enter

Roller skater	Mum! Where are you? Can you take me to the rink?
Swimmer	Dad! Where are you? It's my night for swimming lessons.
Party goer	Mum! Dad! The party starts in ten minutes. I'll do my homework when I get back. Honest.
Judo expert	*(pretends to practise)* I'm ready. And can we pick Richard up on the way there? He says his mum's gone to a disco or something daft.

They all realise no-one's answering; stop what they're doing and gather together

Skater	Do you hear the sound of a car engine?
Children	No.
Swimmer	Do you hear the jangle of car keys?
Children	No.
Party goer	It's very quiet, isn't it?
Children	Yes! Spooky.

There is a knock at the door and another letter is delivered

Judo expert	*(reads letter)*
	Dear all,
	I've decided to go away
	I'm sure you'll manage for just one day
	I'll be back quite soon I'm sure
	Don't forget to lock the door!
	Love Dad.

Skater	But I'm meeting Helen in five minutes!
Swimmer	It's my fifty metres today. I've got to go!
Party goer	It's the social occasion of the year!
Judo expert	What will Richard think?

All	It's not fair!
	When it happens
	We'll not be there!

All go into a group and sulk; enter group of children piling through the door – all stop and look around in amazement

Children	We've been robbed!
Child 1	We've been burgled!
Child 2	We've been ransacked!
Child 3	What a tip.
Child 4	They've been through everything.
Child 5	Turned the house upside down.
Child 6	They must have been here hours to make so much mess.
Child 7	I hope they're not here now!

Children look around nervously

Child 1	Wait a minute. I've just had a thought.
Children	Never!
Child 1	We haven't been burgled. The house is exactly as we left it this morning. It's just that nobody has tidied it up!
Child 2	Don't be silly. It couldn't have been such a mess. It's never normally like this when we get in.
Child 3	That's because someone usually tidies it.
Child 4	And that someone isn't here now.
Children	Mum! Where are you?

There's another knock at the door and another letter is delivered

Child 6	*(reads letter)* Dear all, We've decided to go away We're sure you'll manage for just one day We'll be back quite soon we're sure Don't forget to lock the door! Love Mum and Dad.
Child 5	But we'll never find anything in this mess!
Child 6	Where's my PE kit? It must be under here somewhere! *(starts throwing everything around)*
Child 4	I need my homework for tomorrow. I'm sure I left it here. Or perhaps it was here. Mum would know.
Children	Mum would know!

All sit down together in a sulk; enter group of children with purses, counting their money

Child 1	Five, ten, fifteen . . . let me start again. Five, ten . . .
Child 2	I still haven't got enough.
Child 3	Well, I can't lend you any. I spent all mine at the tuck shop.
Child 4	And don't forget there's your entrance fee for the school disco tomorrow.
Children	*(slap heads)* Oh no! I forgot! Mum! Dad!
Child 5	Our purses are quite empty Our piggy banks are low
Child 6	We need some extra pennies For tomorrow's school disco.
Child 1	You've heard of Cinderella She was magicked to the ball
Child 2	But even mice and pumpkins Won't get us in the hall.
Child 4	Can you hear the sound of money jangling?
Children	No.
Child 3	Can you hear the sound of fivers fluttering?
Children	No.

There's another knock at the door, the children open up to a line of people demanding money, each one carries a token of their job, i.e. a milk bottle, a newspaper, a bucket, etc

Milkman [or woman]	Good evening Hope you're feeling well It's warm again today. Three pints of milk six times a week That's twenty pounds to pay!

Newsboy [or girl]	It's Friday night I'm in a rush I'm going on a trip. One pound eighty is the rate And don't forget my tip!
Window Cleaner	See them shine I've cleaned them well Took longer than it oughtta. That's fifteen pounds for extra time Won't charge you for the water!
All three	Cough up! Pay up! Give us our money! We might be pressed To re-possess If you don't pay us sonny!

The three stand there menacingly

Children	Time to call in some friends. *(they pick up telephones and pretend to dial)* Anyone home?
Group 1	No! We're home alone!
Children	Anyone home?
Group 2	No! We're home alone!
Children	Anyone home?
Group 3	No! we're home alone!

All children in the production stand up

Children	This is most peculiar We really can't believe That all our loving parents Are absent without leave. Whatever we have done to them It was really just in jest We need them back
Group 4	And pretty quick Or they'll charge us all interest!

Enter parents looking absolutely exhausted and bedraggled; they collapse in a heap

Children	Where have you been until this time?
Group 1	You could have phoned!
Group 2	We've been worried sick!
Group 3	And hungry . . .
Group 4	And miserable . . .
Group 1	And lonely . . .
Traders	And we're off . . .
Milkman	I can't stand family arguments.

Window Cleaner	Me neither. There's always kissing and hugging at the end. Ever so. . . soppy!

Traders leave

Parent 1	That was awful!
Parent 2	Pardon?
Parent 1	It was awful.
Parent 2	No, actually, I'm quite empty.
Parent 1	*(goes right up to Parent 2 and shouts)* I said it was awful!
Parent 2	All right, all right! No need to shout. It was just those dreadful loudspeakers. Boom, boom, boom in my ears all night. Now I can't hear a thing.
Parent 3	And the dancing . . . well . . .
Parent 4	Call that dancing? Now, in my day, we had 'Saturday Night Fever' and what about the Bay City Rollers – now that was music! But that . . .

Parents suddenly notice their children staring at them

Child 1	Where have you been?
Parent 1	Out clubbing.
Child 2	Well, you should be ashamed of yourselves, at your age. There's no wonder you're going deaf.
Parent 2	Well, we thought, seeing as no-one's bothered about us here, then we might as well go out and enjoy ourselves.
Parent 3	Trouble was, things have changed a little since we were young.
Child 3	Not half!
Parent 4	We didn't recognise any of the music.
Parent 5	We couldn't dance to any of our favourite tunes.
Parent 6	And now ... I don't know about you, but ...
Parents	I think it's time for bed!
Group 1	What about our tea?
Group 2	What about our trips out?
Group 3	What about the mess this place is in?
Group 4	What about settling a few debts?
Parents	*(turn and look at each other)* Did you hear anything? Me? Not a thing? Night night everyone! *(they exit)*
Children	Parents! What would we do without them? *(look at each other with sudden realisation)* Hang on! Wait for us!

War journeys

Purpose: This script was written for an area assembly involving 60 children following a 'Britain since the 1930s' topic. It was intended to demonstrate a variety of different journeys made by one family during the war years.

Summary: The time navigator acts as narrator, reviewing with a family some of their experiences during the war. The father reflects on his involvement in the Jarrow march prior to the war. One sketch shows sons leaving parents, another sketch includes evacuees placed with some reluctant families. In one sketch, the eldest daughter in the family is shown arriving at a farm as a land girl. The two final sketches demonstrate the whole family reacting to the air raid siren and the return of soldiers from the war.

Approximate running time: 20 minutes – although the air raid sketch has the potential for a script of its own and much more detailed coverage. Additional sketches could be included.

Number of speaking parts: 28 parts, although some of the evacuees speak in unison rather than having individual parts. The time navigator has the largest part and, as the link person, requires a confident speaker with a good sense of timing.

Number of potential parts: The play was performed by 60 children altogether. Additional roles were taken by children joining in during the air raid siren sketch.

Prop requirements: An old-fashioned radio for the family to sit around would be an advantage. A tape of Neville Chamberlain's speech and of an air raid siren are also necessary – although these could both be improvised with percussion instruments and a child reading out the speech. Banners for the Jarrow march would also add to the presentation.

Level of child intervention/adaptation: Children might like to suggest additional lines in the evacuee sketches and/or other characters who might have particular preferences for the child(ren) they would like to foster. There is scope for additional quotes during the soldiers' homecoming and sub-sketches during the Jarrow march, e.g. complaints about blisters.

War journeys

The play is set at the beginning of the second world war; a family is sat around the wireless listening to Neville Chamberlain's announcement

Navigator	*(to the audience)* Don't worry, there isn't really a war just about to start. I'm the time navigator and I've just taken you back in time to 1939, just before the second world war. This family have just finished their tea. They live in **Coventry** [or wherever the play needs to be set]. They've never left the town until now. What they don't realise yet is that the start of the war will mean they will all make some long journeys. Journeys they would never have dreamed about, and journeys that they will wish they didn't have to make.
Dad	*(father in the family unfreezes and addresses the navigator)* You're wrong about one thing son *(navigator turns around with a jump)* I have left Coventry before. I joined a march once. A very long march down to London when we didn't have any work. Well, I'll show you . . .

Large group of children march on with banners; they could chant or even stop and make speeches; the father from the seated family group joins on at the end – marchers exit from the stage

Navigator	So, Dad had left Coventry before. But now, like lots of other fathers, he had to leave again. Some of the fathers and sons were leaving for good.

Enter group of mothers and sons – mothers are fussing as their sons prepare to leave – sons are rather embarrassed by the attention

Mum 1	Have you got enough socks, do you think?
Son 1	Yes Mum.
Mum 2	Have you remembered to pack all your vests?
Son 2	Yes Mum.
Mum 3	Have you got plenty of changes of *(looks around, embarrassed)* you know . . .?
Son 3	Shh . . . we don't want everyone to hear.
Mum 4	Don't forget to write, will you?
Son 4	Yes Mum . . . I mean, no Mum.
Mums	Have you . . .?
Sons	Yes Mum!
Mums	Did you . . .?
Sons	*(impatiently)* Yes Mum!

Enter the train driver to 'lead' the sons off stage

Train driver	All aboard *(blows whistle – sons pretend to open the doors, get in and lean out of the windows to wave)*
Mums	*(all get hankies out and start to cry as sons mime the motion of the train leaving the station and exit from stage)* What shall we do without them?

Exit mothers

Navigator	And so the war meant many men left their homes and went on long journeys. But not only the men disappeared. So did many of the children . . .

The family unfreezes and becomes the centre of the action; the children address their questions to the audience and time navigator

Son	Did I have to go?
Daughter	What happened to me?
Navigator	Both of you were evacuated – that is left the city to live in **Kenilworth** [again, change town if necessary] where fewer bombs were landing. It was thought to be safer. You were all taken to the old school with your teachers and then down to the train station. Just like your father and older brothers. You left Coventry on the train to arrive in the country and be claimed by new families. It wasn't always very pleasant, and sometimes both the children and their new homes got rather a surprise.

Enter evacuee organiser, leading on potential guardians, and evacuees who then stand patiently (or mostly patiently) in line; the son and daughter from the family join the evacuees

Organiser	If you would like to step this way, ladies and gentlemen, we have a group of children just arrived from Coventry.
Child 1	*(an ill-mannered evacuee who stands behind the organiser and imitates him or her)* Just arrived from Coventry.
Organiser	They are a rather motley crew and some look a little worse for wear *(looks angrily at the mimicking child)*.
Child 1	. . . worse for wear.
Organiser	*(looks around angrily)* But I'm sure you'll find someone who will fit into your household perfectly. If we could start with you, Mr Haystack?
Haystack	I need one with plenty of muscles. *(to evacuees)* Hold up your arms *(children do as he asks)* – no that won't do. How about this one? *(chooses a child)* Looks a strong, healthy chap. And this one an' all. *(chooses another)* These'll do. I don't have to feed 'em an' all, do I?
Organiser	We would appreciate it, Mr Haystack. I hear they work better if they're fed.
Haystack	Thought' there'd be a catch somewhere. Come on then, young 'uns. Let's be 'aven you. We've some cows to milk afore supper time.
Organiser	Mrs Lettuce, if you'd like to come this way *(leads one of the adults to the mimicking child)* . . . there's a very interesting looking child *(tries to push the child forward)*
Lettuce	Ooh, no thank you. *(she chooses two of her own)* Now, these two look like they could do with stocking up on a few greens. There's nothing wrong with them that a few cabbages and runner beans won't put right. *(to the children)* Shops closed and I'm boiling up some cabbage for supper.
Children	*(look aghast)* Yuck! *(exit with Mrs Lettuce)*
Organiser	Mr Hardcane. How about this . . . *(once more tries to push*

	forward the troublesome child)
Hardcane	Now, I'm looking for some educated young children who will benefit from a little Latin grammar, and Greek, and Roman history. *(turns to audience)* My specialisms you know. *(turns to children)* Now, these two look pretty clever to me. You are lucky we've got a few hours until the blackout. Just enough time to practise some Latin verbs in your primers.
Children	What? *(exit with Mr Hardcane looking totally confused)*
Organiser	And last but not least, Miss Softsoap. Can I . . . *(tries to push the child forward again)*
Softsoap	Oh! Now I'm all of a flutter. I just can't make my mind up. They're all so gorgeous. Oh . . . *(she chooses some children)* but just look at their clothes! Oh, I shall have a spot of sewing to do I can see . . . tut, tut. What do their mothers think they're playing at? No, come along, a lovely warm bath's already waiting. Well, actually, it might be a bit cold by now . . .
Children	Bath? But it's not Christmas! *(they leave with Miss Softsoap)*
Organiser	*(only the naughty child remains)* Oh dear. Left till last. And it seems we have no more . . . Well, I suppose I'll just have to take you home myself.

Both look equally unhappy at the prospect and exit from the stage

Navigator	Unfortunately, things didn't always go to plan. When the children arrived at their temporary homes, both children and carers found they sometimes did not see eye to eye.

Organiser returns to stage with reluctant child still in tow; adults gradually re-emerge with their lists of complaints and children; Mr Haystack knocks and enters

Organiser	Yes Mr Haystack? How can I help you? Nothing wrong I hope?
Haystack	Wrong? I should say so! It's these farmhands tha's given me.
Organiser	They're actually evacuees.
Haystack	Well, whatever they are, they can't tell one end of a cow from t'other.
Child 2	But we soon found out, Mr Haystack.
Haystack	Aye, only when it lifted its tail up and did its business. They'd only stacked 50 bales and they was complaining of blisters.
Organiser	Well, I do think 50 bales is . . .
Haystack	Aye, I can't believe it mysen. Anyhow, I wants to trade 'em in.

Children are seated next to the organiser; Mrs Lettuce enters next

Organiser	Ah, Mrs Lettuce. How can I help you?
Lettuce	They don't like sprouts! Can you believe it? They don't like sprouts! I got them home for a little stewed cabbage and they wouldn't have that either. Asking for jam and bread they are. Well, I says there's no jam and bread here and, with that, they started crying and asking for their ma! Diabolical I call it. I can't be having young 'uns who don't like vegetables. I want to swap!

Children sit next to organiser

Children	We want our ma!

Bang at the door – this time from Mr Hardcane

Organiser	*(wearily)* Not again. Oh, hello Mr Hardcane. You're not having problems too are you?
Hardcane	Too? Too? They can't count to one, let alone two! I tried them with a little Latin and a few simple pages of number work, and they just sat there for a whole hour. They have no idea. What do they teach them in these city schools? How can we progress to the rise and fall of the Roman empire if they can't count to ten?
Organiser	Come, come. You're surely exaggerating. Why . . .
Hardcane	I demand a transfer. I specifically asked for intelligent children. These will not do!

Children go to sit with the organiser; there is a timid knock at the door and Miss Softsoap enters

Organiser	I don't believe it. Not more problems?
Softsoap	Oh it's a tragedy. It's shameful. The poor bairns. Absolutely covered in bruises, lice and all manner of little beasties. And their clothes! Disgraceful they are. I cannot believe anyone could . . . oh dear . . . I don't suppose you've got any slightly cleaner versions?
All	Send them home! Send them home! We're just not getting on. The best place for all these bairns Is back home with their mom.

Everyone freezes. The son and daughter from the seated family have played two of the evacuated children, come forward and address the time navigator

Children	Did we? Did we go back home?

A third child, an older daughter from the family, leaves her seat and comes forward to address the time navigator

Sister	What about me? What was my journey?
Navigator	You helped the war effort as a land girl. You travelled just like your younger brother and sister and dad on a train. And arrived at Badblister Farm. You thought working on a farm would mean feeding calves and stroking lambs, but I'm afraid . . .

Enter Mr Muckout while villagers and evacuees leave; children return to family

Muckout	Where's me help then? I was told I'd be getting a farmhand and to meet them at the station. I can't see no one! *(looks around)*
Sister	It's me. I'm your land girl. I've come to help on the farm.
Muckout	What? A little lass? But you're nowt but skin and bone. You'll be neither use nor ornament. Tha'd better go back where tha' came from. It's help as I'm wanting, not a little babby.
Sister	I can't go back. I've got to do my bit for the war effort. Please Mr

	Muckout, I'm stronger than I look.
Muckout	Well, if that's the case, tha'd better come with me. See this pile o' muck? *(gestures; girl nods)* That'll need shifting. Here's your fork and after you've finished there'll be cows to milk and the bull could do with mucking out an' all. *(girl looks confused)* What's up lass?
Sister	Excuse me Mr Muckout, but which is the bull?
Muckout	Don't they teach you 'owt in them schools? By 'eck, what's the world coming to?

Girl returns to family while Mr Muckout exits; time navigator tums to the mother in the family

Navigator	And lastly to you, Mum.
Mum	I hope I didn't have many long journeys to make. Otherwise there'll be no one left at home.
Navigator	You had some short, regular journeys. Often at night. Sometimes in your dressing gown. They went something like this . . .

Air raid warning sound; family mime reaction – leaving the house, entering a shelter and waiting for the all clear when they return to their original place on the stage, along with dad

Family	We're fed up We are depressed What misery's in store? Aren't any journeys pleasant That we made in the war?
Navigator	Don't worry, don't worry! Because there was one pleasant journey that many – but not all – were able to make. This was the journey home.

Sons come running on and shake the mother's hand

Son 1	We're coming home.
Son 2	We're coming home.
Son 3	We're coming home.
All	There's no place like home.

All join together in a song associated with the second world war

I'm Henry VIII – honestly!

Purpose: This is a short play, taking a light-hearted look at how Henry VIII turned from a youthful, energetic prince to the image usually portrayed in history books. It is useful for classes and year groups studying the Tudor period and does raise some more serious questions and issues which could be tackled within the history and/or PSHE curriculum.

Summary: Henry VIII introduces himself to the audience, who are rather surprised to discover that he is not the vastly overweight king they are used to seeing in the history books. Henry begins to explain that a mixture of rather indulgent banqueting and the pressure of living with six wives has resulted in his large frame and aged appearance. A range of food is brought on to the stage to a version of *The Twelve Days of Christmas*, and each wife begs a prediction from Mystic Meg as to whether they will produce the son and heir that Henry so desires. In the end, Henry's wives get their own back on the king.

Approximate running time: Quite a short play – approximately 10 minutes – but there is potential for extending it by adding additional scenes.

Number of speaking parts: There are 19 speaking parts with two non-speaking parts.

Number of potential parts: There is a flexible number of monks who come on as a group. Additional scenes could be added by the children involving other ways in which Henry's lifestyle gradually altered his appearance. For example, the 'stress' of frequent battles and arguments with the French and the Scots could be used.

Prop requirements: This play does benefit from some period costumes, particularly for Henry. If possible, at least a few token, plastic ducks and hens during the banquet will add to the visual appeal of the play. A screen or curtain where the characters can be removed for their beheading is needed. The children might be able to make some suggestions themselves for how the headless queens might appear. This can be a good problem-solving activity.

Level of child intervention/adaptation: Additional scenes could be written into this by the children as suggested above. Henry's unhappiness at the sinking of the *Mary Rose* might provide another scene, as could his anxiety over traitors and the instability of his throne at different times during his reign.

Other comments on presentation: Producing the meals that the king is presented with could become a design & technology activity for other children in the year group.

I'm Henry VIII – honestly!

Enter Henry VIII – not looking at all like Henry VIII – accompanied by some children

Henry	Good evening to you all. I'm Henry VIII and I do hope you are enjoying your evening's entertainment. You look a little surprised . . .
Child 1	You don't look like Henry VIII.
Henry	I can assure you, young **man** [or lady] that I am.
Child 2	But Henry VIII was fat!
Child 3	Very fat.
Child 4	This fat . . . *(walks around the stage with a pillow under his shirt – others laugh at him)*
Henry	Well, perhaps I did put on just a little bit of weight in my later years.
Child 1	Just a little bit?
Child 2	A ton more like!
Henry	What cheek! It's very difficult, you know, when you have to go to banquets every day and everybody wants to feed you their finest foods.
Child 3	Chance would be a fine thing!
Cook 4	*(enters and bangs the gong)* Your Royal Highness. The banquet is now ready to be served.
Henry	What's on the menu today then?

Cooks come on to the stage and put down the plates on a table in front of King Henry; they sing to the tune of The Twelve Days of Christmas

Cooks	On the first day of each week, King Henry had for tea . . .
Cook 1	A partridge stuffed with French Brie. *(puts the food in front of Henry and walks off)*
Cooks	On the second day of each week, King Henry had for tea . . .
Cook 2	Two dead ducks . . . *(brings on the food and slaps it down in front of Henry)*
Cook 1	And a partridge stuffed with French Brie. *(picks the food up and slaps it down again)*
Cooks	On the third day of each week, King Henry had for tea . . .
Cook 3	Three roast hens . . . *(brings the food on)*
Cook 2	Two dead ducks . . . *(slaps the food down again in front of Henry)*
Cook 1	And a partridge stuffed with French Brie. *(picks the food up and slaps it down again)*
Cooks	On the fourth day of each week, King Henry had for tea . . .
Cook 4	Four boiled birds . . .
Cook 3	Three roast hens . . .
Cook 2	Two dead ducks . . .
Cook 1	And a partridge stuffed with French Brie.
Cooks	On the fifth day of each week, King Henry had for tea . . .
Cook 5	Five blackbird pies.
Cook 4	Four boiled birds . . .
Cook 3	Three roast hens . . .
Cook 2	Two dead ducks . . .
Cook 1	And a partridge stuffed with French Brie.

Cooks	On the sixth day of each week, King Henry had for tea . . .
Cook 6	Six jugs of cider . . .
Cook 5	Five blackbird pies.
Cook 4	Four boiled birds . . .
Cook 3	Three roast hens . . .
Cook 2	Two dead ducks . . .
Cook 1	And a partridge stuffed with French Brie.
Cooks	On the seventh day of each week, King Henry had for tea . . .
Cook 7	Seven salted seagulls . . .
Cook 6	Six jugs of cider . . .
Cook 5	Five blackbird pies.
Cook 4	Four boiled birds . . .
Cook 3	Three roast hens . . .
Cook 2	Two dead ducks . . .
Cook 1	And a partridge stuffed with French Brie.
Cooks	On the eighth day of each week King Henry –
Henry	Hold it!
Cooks	Hold what?
Henry	Hold the banquet!
Cooks	Why?
Henry	First, because I can't eat any more than this, and second because . . . there aren't eight days in the week.
Cook 1	But our song has twelve days!
Henry	Idiot. How can you have twelve days in the week?
Cooks	But . . . but . . .
Henry	Executioners . . . the cooks are arguing with me! Chop off their heads!

Two executioners chase them behind a screen and one at a time the cooks scream; the executioners emerge with a basket of chopped heads

Henry	So that's why, by the end of my reign, I looked a little larger than at the beginning.
Child 2	But how come you ended up with so much grey hair and so many wrinkles?

Enter Henry's six wives

Catherine A	Where is that good-for-nothing husband of mine . . .?
Anne B	Missing as usual. Always out hunting he is these days.
Jane	No good around the palace, he isn't. And the amount he eats . . . well . . .
Anne C	And he calls me ugly.
Catherine H	I know. Charming, isn't he? And he's definitely past his sell-by date.
Catherine P	Sold out long ago if you ask me!
Henry	Nag, nag, nag. From morning till night. Just imagine having six wives! There's no wonder I turned old and grey before my time.
Wives	Ooh, listen to him, will you!
Catherine P	Yes, but you didn't have to live with us all at the same time!
Anne B	No. Your executioners saw to that.
Henry	Thank goodness I did get rid of a couple of you. Can you imagine the stress I would have been under otherwise?
Catherine H	Some men don't know when they're well off!
Henry	Well, I know I can only cope with one of you at a time.

Wives	But which one will it be?
Catherine A	But then again, we all know he's only after one thing . . .
Wives	A SON!
Henry	But which one is destined to bear me a boy? I haven't got that much time left and I can't put up with the lot of you much longer!

Enter Mystic Meg with her crystal ball

Mystic Meg	On Wednesdays and on Saturdays You wouldn't stand a chance. But seeing that it's **Tuesday** [or whenever] I'll advise you in a glance.
	I'll look into my mystic ball And gaze upon what's there. The future laid out on a plate I'll predict your son and heir.
Catherine A	*(throws herself down at the fortune teller's feet)* Surely it's me. Catherine of Aragon who will bear the son his highness so desperately desires.
Child 2	*(to the audience)* She's a bit keen, isn't she?
Mystic Meg	The sons you had were all diseased And Henry, no remorse. For all you did your very best It ended in divorce.
Henry	*(gives Catherine of Aragon her suitcase)* So long! *(Catherine leaves in tears)*
Anne B	Please tell me my fate. Surely I, Anne Boleyn, must have given him a son?
Mystic Meg	Oh Anne, so very pretty A daughter came instead. You strayed a little in your love And promptly lost your head.
Anne B	My head? Oh no! *(the executioners take her behind the screen; she screams)*
Jane	Please tell me, did I have any better luck?
Mystic Meg	It's true you bore the king a son But gave your life instead. Within a week your time was done You're well and truly dead.

She swoons and is carried off stage

Anne of Cleves enters and babbles

| Mystic Meg | Oh dear, oh dear dear Anne of Cleves
You look just like a horse.
Old Henry wasn't too impressed |

It ended in divorce.

Anne of Cleves leaves the stage in tears

Catherine H	I'm sure I charmed the old goat, didn't I?
Mystic Meg	You charmed our Henry, certainly As he was by then much older. But ended up without a link Between your head and shoulder.

Catherine Howard is taken behind the screen and executed as before

Catherine P	Then that leaves me. I knew I'd win!
Mystic Meg	Yes it's true and celebrate There wasn't any other. But the ending isn't good You weren't to be a mother.
Henry	You mean I paid out for all those weddings, had to make friends with all those mothers-in-law, and still didn't end up with a healthy son and heir?
Mystic Meg	No, but we've had fun talking about you ever since! Anyway, unless there's anything else . . .?
Henry	Well actually, I've placed a little bet on a jousting competition at Hampton Court. The 3.30 this afternoon. Any chance of a . . .?
Mystic Meg	Considering what happened to your wives, I think I'll give that little prediction a miss. *(exits)*
Child 1	Why not just accept that you will always be remembered for being a slightly podgy person and for having six wives?
Henry	But it's so unfair! I did so many other things. I closed down so many monasteries.

Monks come running across the stage

Monks	You can't do that!
Henry	I did. And I spent a lot of time perfecting my torture routine on anyone who said 'you can't do that'.
Monks	*(suddenly change their minds)* You can! you can! With pleasure . . . here's the treasure. *(go off stage and return with a treasure chest)*
Henry	*(opening it up)* Well, I suppose there were a few compensations.

Enter Anne Boleyn and Catherine Howard with their heads tucked beneath their arms

Henry	*(obviously nervous)* Well, well ladies. Fancy seeing you here.
Wives	Fancy! *(they are getting closer and closer, menacingly)*
Henry	Nice day, isn't it?
Anne B	Can't say as we've noticed.
Catherine H	In fact, I think we've only got eyes for you. Oops, sorry. I don't have any eyes any more seeing as I don't have a head.

| Anne B | There seems to be a funny smell around here. Reminds me of that smelly old king I used to live with. But of course, I couldn't possibly be smelling him seeing as I don't have a head. |
| Henry | Now, now. There's no need to be like that. We can all be friends, can't we? |

All wives return to stage

Wives	Henry VIII, it's time that we showed
	The strength of our feelings for you.
	For you didn't care what you did to our hearts
	And you broke every one in two.
	Now we've returned for a little pay back
	and though it's not what we've read.
	We've decided it's time that you hit the deck
	EXECUTIONERS – OFF WITH HIS HEAD!

The Sinking Rat

Purpose: This is a long, fairly complex play that was written for performance by 60 Year 6 leavers. It was an end-of-year production and aimed to be fun and give everyone chance to have a speaking part.

Summary: The events centre around an old-fashioned sailing ship called The *Sinking Rat*. Around this central focus there are several small sets: a kitchen; a news room; a police station. Several characters – a stowaway; a kidnapped boy and his kidnappers; and a group of rats (who take on the role of journalists) – find themselves variously sheltering on board the ship.

They become witnesses to the undercover dealings of the rogue ship's captain who is plotting to overthrow the ship's crew with the help of a band of pirates, and steal the property he is responsible for on board. In the end, the captain's plot is discovered and the stowaway and kidnapped child save the day. It is a light-hearted production with plenty of opportunity for loud and exuberant characterisation. It culminates in a custard pie.

Approximate running time: 45 minutes.

Number of speaking parts: The play was designed for 60 children. The children are organised into groups of approximately six or seven. These include: a group of pirates; rats; kidnappers; police; and sailors. There are 11 main characters. The principal character of the captain needs a particularly strong individual to make the most of the 'baddy' potential.

Prop requirements: This play does benefit from some effective scenery. The main ship can be represented quite simply by a sail, ship's wheel and other tokens on a raised platform. Some boxes to represent hiding places for the stowaway and kidnappers are also necessary. The most difficult scenic challenges are the smaller sets. Again, these can be represented by tokens, e.g. a breakfast table for the kitchen; a typewriter for the newsroom; a barred window or a police helmet for the police station.

Several smaller boats are also needed to bring characters to and from the main ship. These boats can be signified by the characters' 'rowing', using cardboard oars.

The kidnappers need flowerpots for their heads and all the characters benefit from the correct dress, e.g. the police officers (helmets); the pirates (eyepatches); and so on. The rats benefit from simple masks.

Level of child intervention/adaptation: There is not much opportunity for adaptation other than where the emboldened text suggests that names and incidents relevant to the context might be included.

Other comments on presentation: This is not a simple play to perform, but with ingenuity, it is lots of fun and the children in the cast really enjoy the fact that they never know from one performance to the next who would get the custard pie!

The Sinking Rat

Scene one

Rats climb on board the ship; throughout the play they are portrayed as unscrupulous newspaper reporters and paparazzi; they carry cameras, etc

Rat King	*(climbs on board ship first and looks around the deck)* Coast is clear It's time to board *(looks at watch)* I can smell trouble to come. *(sniffs around – beckons to the other rats)*
Rats	*(climb on board and circle around King Rat)* Trouble trouble We love trouble Let's take some photos at the double.
Rat King	Whenever there's a problem looming Whenever there's a scandal to report We'll be lurking in the shadows Our zoom lenses have you . . .
Rats	Caught! Trouble trouble We love trouble Let's take some photos at the double.
Rat King	Whenever you're up to mischief And not doing just as you ought Just check over your shoulder Our zoom lenses will have you . . .
Rats	Caught! Trouble trouble We love trouble Let's take some photos at the double
Rat King	Can you smell it boys?
Rats	Ahhhh!
Rat King	Can you smell it boys?
Rats	Ahhhh!
Rat King	The smell of trouble is growing Misery, mayhem and vice We'll have them all framed in a picture And sue them for ten times the price!
Rats	Trouble trouble We love trouble This ship is better than we thought With our cameras at the ready Our zoom lenses will have you . . .

King Rat	Caught! *(runs off stage laughing)*

Scene two

Dad is sat at the breakfast table reading the paper; Mum is looking out of the window while washing up

Dad	Dreadful news, love.
Mum	Oh aye?
Dad	Dreadful news. Mortgage rates are up.
Mum	That's nice love *(obviously not listening; looking through the window)* If that cat sits on my begonias again, I'm going to complain to the council.
Dad	Dreadful news. Crime rate is rising.
Mum	That's good, love. I'm sure she doesn't feed it properly. Maybe I should tell the RSPCA.
Dad	Dreadful news. **Coventry** [or another local team] relegated to the third division.
Mum	Ooh, haven't they done well!

Rosy enters

Rosy	I've got some really good news, Mum, Dad.
Mum & Dad	Have you dear? *(obviously not interested)*
Dad	Dreadful news. Heir to **Pountney** [or another relevant name] millions is kidnapped.
Mum	That's nice dear. Oh look, she's coming over to get it. I might just go out and give her a piece of my mind.
Rosy	I said! I've got some really good news!
Mum & Dad	Never mind love. Put a plaster on it.
Rosy	*(to the audience)* It's always the same! They don't listen to me! I just might as well Run away to the sea They'd never notice me gone I'll hide in the hold And eat ship's biscuits Until I get old.
Mum & Dad	Did someone say something? *(look at each other; look at the audience; turn back to what they were doing)*
Rosy	There's a ship leaving port It's sailing today I've packed all my bags And I'm running away It's a really posh vessel All royalty aboard It's easy to hide Where the cargo is stored.
Mum & Dad	Did someone say something? *(look at each other; look at the

audience; turn back to what they were doing)

Rosy	I'll slip out the back Or maybe the front All Dad does is read All Mum does is grunt I'm a nuisance to know They won't miss my face I eat far too much And I clutter the place.
Mum & Dad	Did someone say something? (*look at each other; look at the audience; turn back to what they were doing)*
Rosy	Here goes! (*picks up and slings a rucksack on her back and tries to attract her parents' attention)* Bye Mum! Bye Dad! I'm going now! I'm going now! Don't wait up! I'm running away to sea. I'll probably be a few years . . . who knows? Maybe more once I've got my sea legs. *(exits)*
Mum & Dad	Funny, could have sworn I heard something. *(both shrug their shoulders and turn back to what they were doing)*

Scene three

Rosy creeps on board the ship with only the rats watching; she addresses the audience

Rosy	Don't tell anyone where I am will you? I'll lie low on here for a while till it sets sail and then . . . then I'll come out and I'll make myself so useful that they'll want me to be a proper member of the crew. *(looks nervous and sounds hesitant)* I'll visit Paris . . . New York . . . London . . . Rome . . . Tokyo. *(starts to look a little happier)* Barcelona . . . Athens . . . Luxembourg . . .
Rats	*(quietly from the side of the stage)* Do you know what you're doing, little girl?
Rosy	Who was that? *(to the audience)* Did you hear anything?
Rats	Do you know what you're doing, little girl?
Rosy	Of course I know what I'm doing. *(to the audience, looking more frightened than ever)*
Rats	*(coming on stage and circling her)* London, New York . . . what a joke Paris, Rome . . . ain't got a hope The most you'll ever see out here Are pirates, slice you ear to ear. *(doing the actions)*

Rosy runs away from them but the rats follow

Rat 1	*(tapping her on the shoulder)* Don't you need your teddy bear, lovey?
Rat 2	Better take your toothbrush.
Rat 3	Here're some plasters for your tootsies.
Rat 4	No . . . she don't need those . . . she needs a . . . pistol *(pulls out a pistol in front of her face)*

Rosy runs away screaming; the rats copy her

Rats	Paris, New York . . . you're not real London, Rome . . . what's the deal? The only walk you'll make this trip Is up the plank and off this ship. *(imitate falling off a plank)*
Rat 5	Do you need your Barbie doll?
Rat 6	Here, better take some medicine in case your tummy aches.
Rat 7	Here we are *(takes out a bottle of sun cream)* factor 25 . . . we don't want your lovely skin to burn.
Rat 4	No . . . she don't need those . . . she needs a . . . cutlass *(pulls out a cutlass in front of her face)*

Rosy runs into the hold to hide

Rats	Where's she gone? Oh dear, oh my She feels a little queasy She's started missing Ma and Pa Running off is not that easy Maybe there's a story here . . . *(get out cameras and notepads)* Trouble trouble We love trouble Let's take some photos at the double! *(they run after her then freeze as they shout)* You've been caught!

One of the rats runs from the ship and takes a photo, hot off the press, to the Rattle and Report *headquarters; this messenger and the newspaper boy remain the link between several scenes*

Messenger	Hold the print, hold the print! We've got a story It'll make a mint!
Editor	Will it, by Jove? Is it sleazy? *(messenger nods enthusiastically)* Is it disgusting? *(messenger nods enthusiastically)* Will it ruin lots of people's lives?
Messenger	Lots of lives.
Editor	Is it completely untrue?
Messenger	Not completely, but I'm sure we could alter some bits.
Editor	*(snatching the article)* We'll print it!

The editor exchanges the article for a newspaper, which he hands to the newspaper boy; the newspaper boy runs around the audience each time before delivering the paper to its intended reader

News boy	Extra! Extra! Read all about it! Stowaway on brand new ship. *(throws the paper to Rosy's parents)*
Dad	*(picks up paper and sits down at the table to read it)* I tell you, one day, I'm going to complain to that boy!
Mum	I should if I were you. Always digging up the roses he is.
Dad	Quite right, Mother. Look at this dreadful news. Stowaway on brand new ship. What's the country coming to?
Mum	There he goes again. Doing his dirty where I was digging only

	yesterday.
Dad	And they still haven't found the kidnapped boy.
Mum	It's very quiet today, don't you think?
Dad	It's very quiet today, don't you think?

Scene four

The kidnappers enter, leading on the kidnapped boy who is manacled; they are disguised as flowers with plastic flowerpots on their heads; the kidnappers are not very bright; however, Ronald Rich, the kidnapped boy, is much smarter and is really quite enjoying the adventure

Kidnapper 1	Are you sure no-one will recognise us?
Kidnapper 2	Course not. If we see anyone, all we have to do is freeze and pretend to be a windowsill of flowers. Shall we practise?
Kidnapper 3	Freeze!
Kidnapper 2	I'm not ready yet, you dimwit!
Kidnapper 3	Sorry.
Kidnapper 1	Freeze!
Kidnapper 4	I wasn't ready then.
Kidnapper 1	Sorry.
Ronald	Tell you what, I'll count you in. On the count of three, one, two, three, freeze! *(all kidnappers assume pose and freeze)*
Kidnapper 4	Ah . . . ah . . . ah . . . chooo!
Kidnappers	That's no good.
Kidnapper 2	We'll be spotted if you go around the place sneezing.
Kidnapper 4	Ah . . . ah . . . ah . . . chooo! I can't help it. I'm allergic to flowers.
Kidnapper 2	Why didn't you tell us?
Kidnapper 4	I didn't want you to be mad at me.
Kidnapper 2	Well I am mad. In fact, I'm going to chop your roots off and pluck out your petals just as soon as I get my hands on you!
Ronald	Gentlemen, gentlemen. This won't do. If you're really going to kidnap me and hide me on this ship, you'd better get a move on before someone sees through your wonderful disguise. My father *(to the audience)*, a very rich and important person I'll have you know, will have his detectives all over town looking for me. *(to the kidnappers again)* If you don't hurry up, your plot to make lots of money out of me simply won't work. I have to say your planning and preparation leave a lot to be desired as it is. In fact, here he comes now . . . freeze!

All of the kidnappers freeze and Ronald ducks down behind them as his parents pass by in front of the stage; they are dressed very grandly

Mr Rich	*(takes out his pocket watch)* Come along dear. Come along. I must check the office for the latest stock market prices.
Mrs Rich	Oh, but Alfred. You did promise we could stop by Harrods on our way there. I really must pick up a little of their finest caviar. I haven't had any for . . . ooh . . . hours.

Mr and Mrs Rich freeze along with the kidnappers; Ronald turns to speak to the audience

| Ronald | Well, I must say. What do you think of that? I've only just been kidnapped and what are my ever-loving parents discussing? Caviar! *(moves to the front of the stage, walks up to his mother, and circles her while she remains frozen)* Please note. No tears streaming from her face. No signs of unhappiness at all. In fact, in fact, I do believe they've forgotten about me already. |

Ronald withdraws to hide again; Mr and Mrs Rich unfreeze

Mrs Rich	*(turning to her husband)* Alfred . . .
Mr Rich	Is it important?
Mrs Rich	It's just, I feel there's something missing.
Mr Rich	Credit cards? Jewellery? Fur coat?
Mrs Rich	No, no. Nothing like that. *(appears to be thinking)* I've got it! What about Ronald? You remember? Our son.
Mr Rich	Oh yes. What an inconvenience. He was kidnapped wasn't he? Well, what about him?
Mrs Rich	Do you think we should just check at the police station, see if he's turned up?
Mr Rich	*(looks at his watch)* Very inconvenient. But it might seem rather suspicious if we don't. Somebody might actually think we wanted him to be kidnapped.
Riches	*(smirking)* What an idea!

Mr and Mrs Rich approach the police station; the police force are fast asleep; Mr Rich rings the handbell; they all jump up and pretend to be busy

Mr Rich	Any sign of my son yet?
Police	*(jumping to attention)* We seek him here We seek him there We seek him anywhere we dare na na na na, na na na, na na. *(making police siren noise)* The boys in blue We'll search the loo We're checking everywhere he knew na na na na, na na na, na na.
Mr Rich	*(to Mrs Rich who is pretending to cry)* Please console yourself my love. Britain's finest police force are on the trail.

Behind them the police officers resume their recumbent positions; Mr and Mrs Rich exit; kidnappers and Ronald unfreeze and move on board the ship

| Kidnapper 2 | Now's our chance . . . all aboard! |

The kidnappers hide between and within crates on the opposite side of the ship to Rosy; at this point they have not met

Scene five

Enter the captain, a ruthless, unkind slave-driver; he bullies the sailors on board the ship

Captain   Bring it on!
Load the ship!
Watch your step!
Get a grip!

Move to your feet!
Up your pace!
Or get a crack!
Across your face!

Captain stands at the front watching as the sailors begin to carry boxes and barrels on board; if a sailor stumbles, he pretends to kick him or her

Crew   Give us a chance
Get off our backs
There's heavy booty
In these sacks.

We'll do our best
Give us a break
We're only human
Our backs ache!
(at last they collapse in a heap)

Captain   What's the matter with you? *(he tries to kick a few but they just roll over and moan)*

1st mate   The lads and lasses are just a little bit tired.

Captain   Tired? Tired!
I'll have you all fired
Or thrown to the sharks
You'll wish you weren't hired!

Crew   We already do!

Captain   Less of your cheek
You must learn your rank
The last crew of mine
All walked the plank.

Crew   *(all jump up, terrified)*
No, not the plank
Please, not the plank!

Captain   Well get to your posts
And best make it fast
Draw up the anchor
And shin up the mast.
(he chases the crew off to their posts in the rigging)

Scene six

Captain   *(to the audience)* Did you see all those boxes? Full of jewels they are . . . and clothes . . . and all kinds of *(rubs hands together avariciously)* rich pickings. Well, those rich pickings are going to be mine! I've had enough of sailing the seas for a miserable pittance. It's time I should retire to a little captain's rest home just off Scarborough. I have friends . . .

At this point a band of pirates enter and 'row' across the stage

Pirates   Ooh ah!
Captain   I have friends . . .
Pirates   Shiver our timbers . . . what friends we be . . .
Captain   And when this ship is far out at sea . . .
Pirates   Aye, aye, landlubbers. When we're at sea.
Captain   They'll jump over rigging and seize all the goods. We'll take a few prisoners and, wham bam! It's in the can! I'll be set for life. Lots of money and no more seasickness.

Pirates pull up alongside the ship, board it and shake hands with the captain

All   But that's just between you and me!

Pirates climb back off ship, but remain close in their boat to the stage; Captain also leaves the ship; Rosy and Ronald speak to the audience separately as do the rats; they are still not aware of each other's existence but have all heard the plot

Rosy   *(stands up)* Did you see that? *(sits down)*
Ronald   *(stands up)* Did you see that? *(sits down)*

Rats   *(stand up)* We saw it
We saw it
We just can't ignore it.

Trouble trouble
We love trouble
This captain's not a pleasant sort
With our cameras at the ready
Our zoom lenses will have him . . .
Caught!

Messenger   *(brandishes an incriminating photograph which he or she runs around to the newspaper editor with)*
Hold the print, hold the print
We've got a story!
It'll make a mint!

Editor   Will it increase sales of our newspaper by 30%?
Messenger   40% easy.
Editor   Does it come from dubious sources?
Messenger   Extremely dubious.
Editor   We'll print it!

Editor hands over the newspaper to the newspaper boy who then proceeds to deliver it to Rosy's parents

News boy	Extra! Extra! Read all about it! Captain linked with band of pirate thugs. *(throws paper to Rosy's dad)*
Dad	*(picks it up and sits at the table to read it)* One day I'm going to buy a dog and sit it right underneath that letter box.
Mum	*(still washing up)* Not a dog? She hasn't bought a dog as well has she? She can't control her cat, never mind a dog. What's the world coming to?
Dad	*(something catches his eye in the newspaper)* Well I never. Who'd have thought it? Captains making friends with pirates. What's the world coming to?
Mum	I wish our Rosy'd make more friends. Funny that . . . can't remember her coming down for her breakfast. Well I never. Would you look at that! She's only putting her washing out in her slippers!
Mum & Dad	What's the world coming to?

Scene seven

Captain and crew are busy on board the Sinking Rat

Captain	All aboard who's going aboard! All aboard who's going aboard!
Crew	*(rush to grab the anchor)* Heave Ho! Heave Ho!

Ship's bell rings, the cast freeze; characters come out one at a time to remind the audience of who they are and what their role is on board ship

Crew	Oh yeah! Oh yeah! Who do we have on board today?
Captain	You've got the captain! Just watch your step. I'm mean, I'm nasty, I'm after your money. I completely untrustworthy, my best friends are pirates. Like to get to know me better, would you?
Crew	No way! No way! Who else do we have on board today?
Rosy	I'm poor old Rosy. The secret stowaway. My parents don't even know I'm gone. I'm harmless, I'm brave. I'm ready for adventure. But I wish now I'd remembered my teddy bear. You haven't got a spare have you?
Crew	No way! No way! Who else do we have on board today?

Ronald	I'm happy Ronald. I've been kidnapped. Happy? Yes, happy. I'm in the middle of an adventure. It's the best thing that's ever happened to me. Usually I'm stuck in my boring old boarding school or following my father to the stock exchange. At last I can get up to real mischief!
Crew	You don't say? You don't say? Who else do we have on board today?
Kidnapper 1	We're a gang of unfortunate crooks. We thought kidnapping was an easy way to make money.
Kidnapper 2	The trouble is, we don't seem to be getting very far collecting our ransom money.
Kidnapper 3	In fact, you might even wonder if his parents want the boy back at all.
Kidnapper 4	We've given them lots of chances to pay up and so far . . .
Kidnappers	Nothing!
Crew	Won't pay! Won't pay! Who else do we have on board today?
Rat King	Deep down in the hold, if you look very hard, you'll see a host of rats. We love trouble and we know we're going to get it. Where else but the *Sinking Rat* with its crooked captain and stashed stowaways could you hope to find so many front-page stories? It's a scoop!
Crew	You don't say? You don't say? Who else do we have on board today? *(the ship falls silent; the crew look around bemused until they suddenly realise . . .)* Why us of course! We're fighting fit and ready We'll hold our course steady Up the rigging and through the breeze We'll scrub the decks on hands and knees.
Captain	*(to the audience)* They'd better!
Crew	We're longing to stop stalling America is calling So up the anchor and out the sails Watch out for icebergs, mermaids, whales. America here we come!
Pirates	*(to the audience)* Perhaps!

Exit pirates; Rat King takes centre stage

| Rat King | *(to the audience)* It's a scoop! It'll make me famous! I can see it now: 'Rat King Uncovers Pirate Plot'. All I have to do is to get some undercover photos of the captain talking to the pirate leader and my future is guaranteed. Even *The Times* will want to hire me. And, if |

I'm not mistaken, the pirate ship is heading this way now.

Rat King ducks down as the pirates re-enter the ship; they row up alongside the ship, the pirate captain boards the ship and speaks to the ship's captain; in the meantime, the rats can be seen by the audience taking photographs of the undercover operation, with Ronald Rich's face peering at the scene in the background; the pirates exit again and one of the rats rushes around to the editor with the story and photographs

Messenger	Hold the print, hold the print We've got a story! It'll make a mint!
Editor	*(reads the story)* Wow! What a scoop. I can see it now! Editor saves the day. Early retirement. Lots of awards. Invited to all the best dinners. We'll print it!

Editor hands a copy of the paper to the newspaper boy who runs around to the police station and hands over the latest edition; the police officers are all sat with their feet up, demanding the paper be passed from one to the other of them

Chief Insp	Pass the paper!
Deputy Insp	Pass the paper!
Police officer	*(grudgingly)* There's your paper.
Chief Insp	Sir!
Deputy Insp	Sir!
Police officer	*(sarcastically)* Sir!
Chief Insp	*(opens paper and starts to read while continuing to give orders)* Make some tea!
Deputy Insp	Make some tea!
Police officer	Do I have to? *(chief and deputy glare at him)* Sir.
Chief Insp	*(suddenly jumps up)* This is it! That's them! *(points at the paper)* In the background, in the picture. Look! Ronald Rich has been captured by pirates!
Deputy Insp	I knew it all along. He's hostage on a pirate ship.
Police officer	I could have told you that. *(others glare at him)* Only after you'd told me it first, of course.
Chief Insp	Well? What are we waiting for? Let's get going!
Police officer	*(looks at his watch)* What? Is it home time already?
Chief Insp	Not home, you idiot. Let's go and arrest these pirates before Mr and Mrs Rich find out where he is. You never know. They've got lots of money. There might be a reward in it for us! *(suddenly all the police officers jump to attention, climb on board their boat and row towards the pirate boat)*

The next scene shows the pirate boat and the police boat rowing towards one another with the police falling out one by one

Scene eight

Police	Delta one, delta one Boatlocated Boat located We can see

	We can see It's as stated It's as stated.
Police 4	Many shifty characters are leaning over stern. Beards and parrots. They are pirates. The boat is going to turn.

As the police boat turns, one officer falls out

Police	We all leaned over and one fell out.
Pirates	There were six instead And the little cop said.
Police 5	Row faster Row faster.
Pirates	So they all rowed faster And one fell out *(one police officer falls out)* There were five inside And the little cop cried.
Police 6	Row faster Row faster.
Pirates	So they all rowed faster And one fell out *(one police officer falls out)* There were four still dry When we heard them cry.
Police 4	Shifty looking pirates, we are arresting you in connection with the abduction of Ronald Rasputin Rich. You are not required to say anything, but anything you do say will be taken down and used as evidence. Take them to the cells!
Pirates	Oh no! Not the cells!
Pirate 1	Call **'Rough Justice'**. [or another similar TV show]
Pirate 2	Call the prime minister!
Pirate 3	Call the president!
Pirate 4	Call me mum!
Pirate 5	We are innocent!
Pirate 6	We've been framed!
Chief Insp	Take them down!

Police board the pirate ship and arrest the pirates and row them back to the station

Scene nine

Pirates are back at the station in a cell; the chief inspector paces up and down with the deputy and a police officer

Chief Insp	Is it true that on the night of the 24th May, you knowingly kidnapped an innocent boy – Ronald Rich – and stole him from the care of his ever-loving parents?

Pirates	Not guilty, your honour.
Chief Insp	*(turns to the deputy)* For the record, the accused pleaded guilty.
Deputy Insp	Guilty!
Police officer	Guilty!
Chief Insp	Is it not true that on the 25th of that same month of May, you did knowingly, against his will, without his consent, and with him screaming and begging for mercy . . .
Police officer	Like this Sir? *(acts out an impression of what might have happened)*
Chief Insp	*(looks away disgusted)* . . . that you did drag young Ronald up a plank and on board that worst of all vessels, the *Sinking Rat*?
Pirates	Not guilty, your honour.
Chief Insp	*(to deputy)* The defendants pleaded guilty.
Deputy Insp	*(writing)* Very, very guilty indeed.
Chief Insp	Well, in that case, and being as there is no conflicting evidence, in other words . . . we've got you good and proper. I hereby pronounce the verdict. Guilty.
Deputy Insp	Guilty.
Police officer	Guilty. But shouldn't we have some witnesses or something?
Chief & dep	Witnesses?
Police officer	Or evidence?
Chief & dep	Evidence?
Police officer	I'm sure at police academy they said something about making a case or finding proof or . . .
Chief Insp	I don't know what they teach them at police academy these days. There's no need for all that. Waste of tax payers' money. We have all the evidence we need. *(points to the newspaper)* Rat King has seen them at it. What more evidence can we ask for?
Pirate 7	Before you lock us up . . .
Chief Insp	What now?
Pirate 7	I have a confession to make.
Chief Insp	What a nuisance. Do you really have to? Is it absolutely necessary?
Pirate 7	I think so Sir. You see, we had nothing to do with the kidnap of Ronald Rich. But we were plotting to invade and capture the *Sinking Rat*, murder the crew in their beds, steal all the jewellery, and throw the bodies overboard.
Chief Insp	What do you think I am? Completely stupid? As if I'd believe a ridiculous tale like that. Try anything to get the sympathy of the jury, they will. Take them away!

Exit police and pirates; action returns to the ship where a mutiny is brewing

Scene ten

Captain	All hands aloft!
Crew	*(all stand back to back with arms folded)* Shan't.
Captain	Well, all hands on deck!
Crew	Shan't.
Captain	All hands in pockets, then, if you must.
Crew	*(relax and put hands in pockets)* Better.
Captain	*(to audience)* I don't know what's the matter with them. I can't get them to do anything I ask. Talk about stubborn. I've tried everything.

Behaviour management. Golden stars. **Exclusion at lunchtime**. [or whatever the school is concentrating on] They're just not interested.

1st mate	We're not budging until you give us what we want.
Captain	I've told you. We're completely out of weevil-free biscuits.
2nd mate	We've heard you've got a whole stock of Cadbury's Creme Eggs in your cabin.
3rd mate	And we shan't move until we get our fair share.
Crew	(move around to address the audience) We've had it up to here We're sick now through and through Our only food for months and months Had been dead beetle stew. (turn to captain, 1st mate prodding him with his finger) But we hear that down below It isn't quite the same A certain someone's eating meat We think that it's a shame. (move back to address the audience again) We've had it up to here We won't take any more Our only drink for weeks and weeks Was used to clean the floor. (turn back to the captain) But we hear that down below The captain is no mug He'll take the rum down from his shelf And pour himself a jug. (they start to approach the captain menacingly)
Captain	(pushed right up against the side) Look, this is taking it too far!
Crew	'Tisn't.
Captain	'Tis.
Crew	'Tisn't.
Captain	'Tis.
Crew	This is taking it too far. (grab hold of him) On the count of three.
Captain	No, no! Have mercy!
Crew	(to the audience) Shall we give him a good ducking in the briny?
Captain	(to audience) It's no good. I'll have to call in the reserves. I didn't want to do it like this but . . . (to the crew) if you insist on behaving like this, I'm calling in my chums the pirates.
Crew	(to one another – looking confused) His chums the pirates? (to the audience) His chums the pirates? Is this true?
Rosy	(jumps up from her hideout on stage) I'm afraid so.
1st mate	Who are you? (they relax their grip and turn to Rosy in surprise)
Rosy	I'm Rosy the stowaway. And I overheard him talking to them.
Captain	And now, you loutish lot of lowlife, I'm going to make you wish you'd never been born. When those pirates arrive, they'll throw any

traitors straight overboard. Plop!

Crew	Plop?
Captain	Maybe even plop, plop!
Crew	Plop, plop?
Captain	Exactly! And now . . . *(gets out his portable telephone and looks at his watch, then says to the audience)* It's okay. It's off peak. Two, two. Two, two. Two, two.

Pirate captain stands up from his place in jail

Pirate	Yes? Pirate captain speaking. How may I help?
Captain	It's the captain. I'm going to give you the code word. All Aboard.
Pirate	All Aboard?
Captain	You remember, fool! It's the code word for invading the ship. You know, you come on board with your cutlasses, pistols and muskets and drive the crew overboard into the sea. you remember? Well, it's time. So . . . *(looks around for them coming)* Strange. I can't see you. Whereabouts are you?
Pirate	Prison.
Captain	Sorry? I don't remember that code word. Prison? Does that mean you're starboard?
Pirate	No, we're in prison.
Captain	You're in prison? *(starts to panic and look about him)* Does that mean you can't come and rescue me with your cutlasses, muskets and pistols?
Pirate	I'm afraid so. All our muskets have been confiscated and the judge is looking at our pistols until further notice.
Crew	*(starting as a whisper that builds up)* Walk the plank. Walk the plank. Walk the plank. Walk the plank. Walk the plank. *(it becomes a chant)*
Captain	Now be reasonable. I'm not all bad. *(really starting to cower in the path of the approaching crew)*
Crew	Yes you are.
Captain	Well, I do have my good points!
Crew	No you don't!
Captain	Well, all right then. I'm mean. I don't have any good points. I eat all the best food on ship but, let's face it, who else are you going to get to be captain? Who else will take all the stick? Steer the ship through storm and trouble? *(becomes increasingly melodramatic)* Pay your national insurance . . .?
Crew	*(looking puzzled)* National insurance?
Captain	And pay into your pension fund?
1st mate	We have a pension fund?
Captain	*(becoming more confident)* These are all things you take for granted. Now who else will do them for you?
2nd mate	I'm sure we can find someone. Rat King! We need you!
Rat King	*(appears from his hideout)* Is there a scandal brewing?
1st mate	No. But we need an advert in your paper for a . . . is your pencil ready? For a kind captain . . .
2nd mate	Who shares his biscuits . . .
Crew 3	Who takes late watch . . .
Crew 4	Who'll climb the rigging . . .
Crew 5	Who'll splice the mainbrace . . .
Crew	Have you got all that?

Rat King passes it to one of the other rats who runs off to the editor

Messenger	Hold the print, hold the print We've got a story It'll make a mint.
Editor	Hmm . . . pension funds . . . ship . . . drowning . . . I'm sure I've read this story somewhere before. [this could be changed to something more topical] Never mind. We'll print it!

The newspaper boy collects the paper and delivers it to Rosy's parents' house

Dad	Here, would you look at this!
Mum	I can't stand these neighbours any longer!
Dad	Dreadful things happening in the world. It's a disgrace. British beef banned . . . national pea shortage . . . [or something more topical] captains wanted desperately. Who'd want to be a ship's captain? Mind you, I don't suppose you'd have many neighbours. In fact, no neighbours at all.
Mum	No neighbours? Did I hear you say no neighbours? *(grabs the paper)* What are we waiting for?

Mum and Dad row across to the ship; newspaper boy delivers paper to Mr and Mrs Rich

Mr Rich	Let's see what the stock market's like today. Oh dear. Now will you look at this? Shares down yet again. It really won't do. I need a challenge. Now, blow me over . . . this could be it. Captain Rich. Yes, I can just see it.
Mrs Rich	What are you talking about?
Mr Rich	It's an advert to be captain of a ship. Just the job for an enterprising young man like me!
Mrs Rich	As long as I get to sit at the captain's table.
Mr Rich	I'll even rename the ship after you!
Mrs Rich	Well, what are we waiting for?

Mr and Mrs Rich row out to the ship

Scene eleven

Both couples are rowing towards the ship looking angrily at each other; they arrive at the side of the ship

1st mate	Who are you? *(leans over the side)*
Mum	I've come about the job.
1st mate	Name?
Mum	Mind your own business. You're as bad as the neighbours.
1st mate	Interests?
Mum	Mrs Goodbody at number 24.
1st mate	Have you ever spliced a mainbrace?
Mum	No, but I've sliced an onion.
1st mate	Are you quick at rigging?
Mum	No, but I know all about climbing plants.

1st mate	Have you brought a reference with you?
Mum	No, I'm afraid I haven't.
Rosy	*(stands up from the back of the ship)* I'll be a reference for her!
Mum & Dad	Rosy! What are you doing here?
Dad	Why aren't you in bed?
Rosy	I haven't been in bed for weeks, as if you'd notice. *(to the crew)* Reference for my mum. In the 12 years I have known her, she has shown absolutely no interest in any occupation whatsoever, other than watching the neighbours and complaining about their cat. I suggest that she is totally unsuitable for a life at sea, and would make every member of this crew miserable.
Mum	Oh Rosy. How could you?
2nd mate	If you'd like to step to the side, we will let you know.
1st mate	*(to Mr Rich)* Who are you?
Mr Rich	I am Mr Rich. I'm surprised you don't recognise me as I'm often in the paper!
Mrs Rich	I am Mrs Rich. Could I check. Does this position include complimentary silverware and are there servants to wait at table?

Crew start to hiss and jeer

1st mate	Have you brought your references, Mr Rich?
Mr Rich	Good gracious, me young man. I don't need references.
Ronald	*(stands up from his hiding place)* I can give him a reference.
Riches	Ronald. What are you doing here?
Ronald	In the 13 years I have known Mr and Mrs Rich, I can honestly say that they have devoted themselves, one hundred percent, to the making of money. They have shown absolutely no interest in any of the human beings connected to them and, as such, are totally unsuitable for a life at sea.
Mr Rich	Oh Ronald. How could you say that about me?
Crew	Oh dear, oh dear, we feel let down The choice is rather poor We think they are more suited To a life based on the shore.
Captain	Told you so!
Crew	We can't decide, we must confer Which of these two we'll pick It looks as though they're both about To be rather seasick.

Both Mum and Mr Rich are sick overboard

Captain	Told you so!
Crew	There is no time, we'll have to choose We must employ the best A presentation will not do Nor psychometric test. Eeny, meeny, miny, mo

Catch a captain by the toe
If he's sick we'll let him go
Eeny, meeny, miny, mo.

In the background, Rosy and Ronald have been plotting together; they both interrupt

Rosy & Ron	Hold it!
Crew	Hold what?
Rosy & Ron	We'll do it!
Crew	Do what?
Rosy & Ron	We'll be the captain.
1st mate	But there's two of you.
Rosy & Ron	We'll job share.
Rosy	I'll do mornings.
Ronald	I'll do afternoons.
Rosy	I'll wash.
Ronald	I'll dry.
Rosy	I'll steer
Ronald	I'll lend a hand.
Rosy	I'll sweep.
Ronald	I'll rid the ship of rats. *(chases off the rats with a broom)*
Rat King	Couldn't I just get a picture of the happy couple?
Everyone	No!

Rats exit

Rosy & Ron	Well?
Crew	You're hired.

Everyone cheers; Mr and Mrs Rich stalk off

Mr Rich	What an ungrateful boy. After all the years we've kept him at public school.
Mum	What an ungrateful girl. After all the years I've ignored her!

Mum and Dad stalk off

Kidnappers	Does that mean that Mr Rich isn't going to pay the ransom, Ronald?
Ronald	*(to the kidnappers)* I tell you what. You can stay on board ship. The old captain will need someone to help him scrub the decks three times a day.
Captain	Three times a day? I think I'd rather walk the plank. *(crew move threateningly towards him)* All right, pass the bucket. *(starts to scrub)*
1st mate	Well, this is looking suspiciously like a happy ending.

All actors move back; the focus is on Rosy who now addresses the audience

Rosy	Just before we all go home
	And have a cup of tea
	We've met a lot of baddies
	In this tale of mutiny.

It's only fair if heroes
Can really show it pays
To be a goody goody
In school leaver plays.

And so I bring a custard pie
And look for someone willing
To decide which of our cast
Has been the perfect villain.

The baddies are brought on one at a time and someone from the audience is then chosen to select who should get the custard pie

Ronald	Will it be villain number one, the captain?
Rosy	Will it be villain number two, the rat king?
Ronald	Will it be villain number three, the pirate captain?
Rosy	Will it be villain number four, Mr Rich?
Ronald	Will it be villain number five, Rosy's mum?
Rosy	Will it be villains number six and seven, the kidnappers?

The battle of Bean and Sprout

Purpose: Written for a school leaver concert, this is a large production for a large number of children. It is aimed for performance by Year 6, but could be adapted for younger children.

Summary: A large supermarket opens up opposite a small greengrocer's. The supermarket managers are determined to put the greengrocers out of business and use all kinds of underhand means to do so. With the intervention of a guardian angel, the greengrocers is saved and all ends happily.

Approximate running time: 45 minutes.

Number of speaking parts: 50 individual parts, but there is potential for more as part of a chorus.

Prop requirements: The main scenery involves a supermarket backdrop and greengrocers shopfront. Boxes, cans or cylinders, a deadly spider, plastic portable telephones, pretend microphone, sacks of vegetables, torches, watches, mops and buckets, flipchart and shopping baskets if possible. The costumes are fairly straightforward and can be put together from fairly basic items, e.g. white coats, suits, aprons, burglar masks. For a large-scale production it should be fairly easy to administer.

Level of child intervention/adaptation: There is little opportunity to alter the script, although there are a number of opportunities for audience participation when a level of improvisation would be welcome.

Other comments: The play includes several pantomime traditions and is quite interactive with the audience invited to join in several times. It should appeal to both young children and adults. The mime sketch will need careful directing if the impromptu telephone call is to have its full effect.

The battle of Bean and Sprout

Enter Russ Sprout and Rhona Bean; they walk up proudly in front of their greengrocer's, Beansprout Green and Regular, *and look admiringly at it; Russ Sprout holds up a trophy*

Russ	We did it Rhona. We did it! We won the 'Greatest Greens' competition for the second year running. Let's celebrate. Tell you what, I'll cook you the most delicious Brussel sprout and lentil soup you've ever had in your life. I'll . . . I'll . . . I'll even add some extra garlic, just as you like it.
Rhona	Wonderful. I'm thrilled, honestly. *(she seems rather subdued)*
Russ	I can't wait to ring my mum. Tell you what, I'll ring my mum and you put the stew on. No, no. On second thoughts, I'd better cut some cabbage first and then I'll mop the shop. Or perhaps I should mop the shop . . . *(notices Rhona is looking rather miserable – tries to grab her hands and dance around with her)*
	We have the champ onions my friend
	Our onions you cannot pretend
	Are less than delicious
	And our beetroots nutritious
	We have the champ onions my friend!
	What's the matter, Rhona? Aren't you pleased we won the competition?
Rhona	I am pleased. It's just, oh, I don't know.
Russ	Yes you do. You're the sensible one. You always know what the matter is.
Rhona	Well, it's just . . . maybe we're celebrating too soon.
Russ	What do you mean, too soon? We've won the competition. Our greengrocer's business is the best. Everyone agrees. Now, let's have less of the bottom lip and celebrate. We have the champ onions my friend . . .
Rhona	I had a dream, a nightmare, last night.
Russ	*(not really listening)* Our onions you cannot pretend . . .
Rhona	Our onions shrank to marbles.
Russ	*(continues singing)* Are less than delicious . . .
Rhona	Our cabbages went completely limp.
Russ	Our beetroots nutritious . . .
Rhona	And as for our beetroot! It was mushy.
Russ	*(suddenly realising)* Mushy beetroot? Who says I sell mushy beetroot? Just wait till I get my hands on them. I'll ring their turnips!
Rhona	You haven't listened to a word I've been saying. It was a dream, I mean, a nightmare.
Russ	*(relieved)* Well then. What are you worrying about, you great, green gooseberry? Why do you always look at the grim side to things?
Rhona	For the same reason you always look at the best side of things and don't see the problems. It's just the way we are.

Rhona and Russ freeze; out come the Always look on the bright sides *and the* Don't count your chickens; *these groups appear at different times during the play – the* Bright Sides *dress up as clowns with smiles on their faces, while the* Count your Chickens *dress as clowns with tearful faces; they reflect the optimistic personality of Russ and the pessimistic personality of Rhona*

Brights	*(stand behind Russ)* We feel good! We feel great! And now is the time to celebrate! Pop the cork! Chuck a bun! Be like Russ *(to Rhona – run around pulling faces and waving bottles in the air)* And have some fun!
Chickens	*(enter and start wagging their fingers, trying to push the Bright Sides off the stage)* We feel bad! We feel rotten! We think that you have forgotten Mortgages, debts and loans Be like Rhona Spread your groans!
Brights	*(push Count your Chickens)* Get a life!
Chickens	*(push Bright Sides)* Grow up!
Brights	Don't be mean.
Chickens	Act your age.

Guardian Angel enters and acts as a narrator to speak to the Bright Sides and the Count your Chickens

Angel	It's about time you all started to act your age. This is absolutely dreadful, squabbling like this. While you're arguing, there are some serious problems looming. And when I say serious, I mean serious.
Chickens	*(looking smug)* Told you so.
Angel	*(looks warningly at them)* Now is not the time for these petty arguments. Have any of you noticed what has just pulled up outside?
Brights	An ice cream van?
Chickens	The bank manager?
Angel	You're both wrong. It's Insaneways Supermarkets Incorporated. And, if I'm not mistaken, they're looking for somewhere to build their next megamarket. It's time we made ourselves scarce.

All exit, except for Rhona and Russ who unfreeze

Russ	I really don't know what you're worrying about, Rhona. Lighten up. Dreams aren't going to stop the most wonderful quality grocers in the world from going on to better things.
Rhona	No, but they might! *(she points to two officials walking up and down the plot next to the greengrocers)*

Rhona and Russ retire to the background as the focus moves to a group of 'managers' who appear on stage with clipboards, briefcases and portable telephones

Mr Sane	Please look closely, gentlemen *(looks irritatedly at Ms Strategy)*, and women, at the proposed new development site.

Master Ways	Blimey, Dad. It would make a great football pitch. Anyone for a game of footy?
Mr Sane	*(looks extremely irritated by the boy, who has turned out to be a great disappointment)* Don't talk drivel, Hubert. Only street urchins play football. It's rugby league for you, and if you can't keep your mind on matters in hand, I'll have to send you home to your mother.
Ms Strategy	If we could return to the matter in hand, Sir. It does look a very good site, I must say. Although I do think we should progress cautiously with the marketing plan. Have we been in touch about planning consent?
Mr Quality	A very important point, Ms Strategy. I was just about to say the same. Marketing plan, that's what we need.
Mrs Monitor	Indeed, Mr Quality. But have we got our performance indicators in place?
Mr Margin	Profit! That's what it's all about. How much money are we going to make?
Mr Sane	Now, just a minute . . . can I remind you who's in charge here?
Managers	You Sir.
Mr Sane	Who makes decisions here?
Managers	You Sir.
Mr Sane	Who pays your wages?
Managers	You Sir.
Mr Sane	Who's always right?
Managers	You Sir.
Mr Sane	What's our motto?
Managers	When you're feeling hungry When you want to scoff Insaneways have the answer We aim to rip you off!
Mr Sane	Yes, quite right too. But what do we tell the customer?
Managers	When you're feeling hungry Your tummy starts to rumble Please stop by at Insaneways You'll never have to grumble!
Mr Sane	I prefer the first one myself.
Master Ways	Dad, why do we have to rip people off?
Mr Sane	*(becomes furious and flies into a paddy, which he does repeatedly)* Why . . . why . . . why . . . What do you mean, why? I cannot believe I could have fathered . . . why . . . why . . . why . . . It is a well-known prime-marketing fact that our chief objective is to rip people off. Our customers expect to be ripped off. They like being ripped off. They enjoy standing in long queues. They like paying through the nose for our own brand products. It's what they've come to expect. It's what they deserve. And it's jolly well what they're going to get . . . *(he works himself up into an increasing fury)*
Ms Strategy	*(rather fed up)* It's time for the smelling salts. *(Mr Quality comes out with the smelling salts and starts to try and calm Mr Sane down)* Repeat after me . . . *(to Mr Sane)* last year's Insaneways profits were up by 600%.
Mr Sane	Profits up 600%.

Ms Strategy	We made half our workforce redundant and replaced them with computers.
Mr Sane	No workforce . . . computers. *(starts to smile)*
Ms Strategy	You were awarded businessman of the year.
Mr Sane	Oh yes . . . of the year. I'm starting to feel much better.
Ms Strategy	And were personally responsible for closing down 6,000 puny little greengrocers.
Mr Sane	Ah, thank you Ms Strategy. I think I can continue now.

A portable phone starts to ring somewhere; all the managers jump to attention and start searching for which phone is ringing

Managers	It's the phone. Who's phone? Which phone? Where phone? It's the phone. Who's phone? Which phone? Where phone?

They become increasingly panicky as the can't find where the ringing is coming from

Mr Sane	Stop! Idiots! Hold up your phones. *(managers get their phones out – Mr Sane goes up to each one; gets to the end and looks puzzled)*
Master Ways	Dad! It's yours!
Mr Sane	Well, why didn't you tell me? What a fool for a son. *(brings out phone and snaps at person at other end)* What do you want? Oh, I see . . . right . . . yes . . . good news . . . good news indeed. *(managers group around trying to listen)* Up by 700% and planning permission? Wonderful. *(to this good news, the managers start dancing around silently, mock cheering; Mr Sane replaces phone)* Another breakthrough for Insaneways! We have planning permission. Building can start straight away.
Master Ways	For a football pitch?
Mr Sane	No, idiot! For our new branch. We can start with the bulldozers tomorrow.
Ms Strategy	Mr Sane, I don't want to put a damper on the festivities, but shouldn't we do a little market research and perhaps assess the competition?
Mr Sane	What competition?
Ms Strategy	Well, if you took the time to look around, you'd notice a rather dingy little greengrocers behind you. I think we should perhaps check out their products and do a little strategic planning for how we make sure they don't affect our profits.
Mr Sane	Mmm. *(walks over to Beansprouts and sniffs)* What a seedy looking little dump. Shouldn't take long to get rid of that one.
Ms Strategy	Which strategy would you like us to use, Mr Sane?
Mr Sane	Just remind me what they are again. I just love to hear all the fiendish ways in which we reduce our competitors to rubble.
Mr Quality	Strategy one – runaway bulldozer plan.
Mrs Monitor	Strategy two – customer poisoning plan.
Mr Margin	Strategy three – takeover with forged bank notes plan.
Ms Strategy	But if I can suggest, Mr Sane, our most successful plan to date has been strategy four – call in the inspectors plan.
Mr Sane	Ah yes. That happens to be my favourite one too. Let me check . . . *(goes into a trance state)* oh cheques, blank cheques, paying in cheques . . .
Ms Strategy	*(clicks her fingers to bring him back down to Earth)* Let me

	recap for you, Sir. Our inspectors' plan included planting a rather large number of deadly spiders in the greengrocer's and tipping off the local food inspectors.
Mr Sane	Oh . . . what a totally wonderful plan. I can leave this plan in your capable hands, can't I Ms Strategy?
Ms Strategy	Oh, completely, Sir.
Mr Sane	(starting to lead them off) Let me hear it once more!
Managers	When you're feeling hungry When you want to scoff Insaneways have the answer We aim to rip you off!

Exit managers, enter a newsreporter with microphone

Reporter	(speaking into the microphone and addressing the audience) And here we are at the site of the new Insaneways Supermarket. Who would have believed that only weeks ago this was a green field with no purpose whatsoever. As I'm sure you'll see at the unveiling of the new store, it is a monumental feat of engineering design and has already been nominated for five Botcher awards for innovative design. And now here comes the master behind that new store.

Enter Mr Sane with managers, followed by a group of shoppers

Ms Strategy	(to the shoppers) Now, you all know what you've got to say, don't you?
Shopper 1	When do we get paid again?
Ms Strategy	Shh. Keep your voices down. It'll arrive in the post. If you make a good job of it of course.
Reporter	And just before the guest celebrity declares the store open, let's speak to a few of their loyal customers. (approaches one shopper) Excuse me, madam. What makes you a regular customer of Insaneways?
Shopper 2	(speaks in a very stilted, formal way – obviously rehearsed) I am a very loyal customer of Insaneways because they are the cheapest by far.
Reporter	(approaches another shopper) And you, sir. Why Insaneways?
Shopper 3	Because Insaneways are the best. They always guarantee rock-solid value for money.
Reporter	And you, madam? What makes their fruit and veg so delicious?
Shopper 4	Because they always serve you with a smile.
Reporter	(looks confused) And what do you think of their dairy products?
Shopper 5	Theirs is the best range of toiletries in town.
Reporter	(still confused) Well, thank you. What better recommendation? Obviously Insaneways have the support of their customers.
Shopper 1	(shouts across to Ms Strategy) Can we go now?
Ms Strategy	Shh! No you can't. There's the presentation yet.
Reporter	(to the audience) And here comes our guest celebrity, **Mr Turner**. [or a staff member's name] (draws back the curtain to reveal the new store; everyone claps except for Russ Sprout and Rhona Bean, who are stood on the stage in the background, and Master Ways)

Master Ways	I always said it would have looked better as a football field.
Reporter	And as the shoppers return home, happy that there is even more local opportunity to buy more, buy better, buy cheaper, you can hear that pleasant little verse of which we are all so fond.
Shoppers	When you're feeling hungry Your tummy starts to rumble Please stop by at Insaneways You'll never have to grumble!

Exit shoppers; exit Rhona and Russ shaking their heads and dragging their feet; the reporter approaches the remaining group on stage – the managers and Master Ways

Reporter	And maybe just a brief word from the hero of the moment, Mr Sane himself! Mr Sane, obviously a very proud day for you?
Mr Sane	*(beams at the camera)* It most certainly is. Store 500. And, as I'm sure you can see, it's a fine design for the 21st century.
Reporter	Yes, indeed. There are one or two locals, I do believe, or so I've heard, who are a little concerned about the effect this may have on other shops in the area. Mr Sane *(smile starts to fade as he goes into a tantrum)* Who? Where? Let me at them. What? How dare . . . I can't believe . . .
Reporter	*(obviously rather worried)* Not me, you understand . . . I . . . I think it's marvellous. I mean . . .
Mr Sane	How dare they! How dare they!
Ms Strategy	Smelling salts! Don't worry Mr Sane. Repeat after me. Profits up 700%.
Mr Sane	Profits up 700%.
Ms Strategy	Nominated for five Botcher awards.
Mr Sane	Only five? Well, I suppose it's better than nothing. Thank you, Ms Strategy. I'm feeling much better now.
Reporter	*(still rather nervous)* Please, Mr Sane, let me help you to your car.

Mr Sane and reporter exit to leave the managers and Master Ways on stage

Ms Strategy	*(they gather around her, the lights dim)* Are we all ready for tonight, then?
Master Ways	The England v Ireland match? I can't wait!
Ms Strategy	No, idiot! Strategy four – planting large numbers of deadly spiders in the greengrocer's next door.
Master Ways	But, isn't that rather underhand, mean and totally against every principle of our country?
Managers	Naturally! Don't forget . . . When you're feeling hungry When you want to scoff Insaneways have the answer We aim to rip you off!

Lights go off – the next scene is largely mime; the managers enter, led by Ms Strategy with her torch; they creep into Beansprouts where there are five bags of labelled vegetables; Ms Strategy hands a box labelled 'poisonous spiders' to Master Ways who drops it; Managers panic, running around picking them up; at last they have them back together; Ms Strategy snatches it back off Master Ways and is just about to put them in a sack when the telephone goes off; they all start panicking; whose phone is it? – pretend to look at the audience

Managers	It's the phone. Who's phone? Which phone? Where phone? It's the phone. Who's phone? Which phone? Where phone?
Ms Strategy	I don't care! Just turn it off. *(all get their phones out and check – one is still ringing; eyes turn to Ms Strategy)*
Managers	It's for you.
Ms Strategy	*(answers phone)* Who is it? I'm in the middle of an important meeting.
Angel	*(off stage)* We're watching you, Ms Strategy Don't count your chickens yet Bean and Sprout are not alone Tonight you will regret.
Ms Strategy	*(looks at now silent phone puzzled)* How strange. Something about counting chickens. *(to other managers)* Well, have you done it yet? *(managers shake their heads, Ms Strategy grabs the spiders from them, tips them in, and they exit – Ms Strategy drops her phone but does not realise)*

Enter Rhona and Russ – they sit in their shop and count money

Rhona	No, it still isn't enough.
Russ	Try again, Rhona. You must have counted wrong.
Rhona	I've already tried ten times. I've used the calculator, the adding machine and lots of mental maths. We just don't have enough this week to pay their wages.
Russ	But we're the best. We must have. *(reaches into a sack, but not one with spiders in)* Just look at the quality of those potatoes. Not a worm in sight. *(picks out of another sack)* And these carrots are second to none. How can we not afford to pay our staff?
Rhona	For goodness sake, Russ. Just look around you. What do you see?
Russ	A shop full of wonderful fruit and veg.
Rhona	And?
Russ	And?
Rhona	No customers. Use your eyes, Russ. We have tomatoes, grapes, aubergines, onions, potatoes and pears. *(picks out of each sack, except the one with spiders in)* And bananas. But no customers. It's ever since that dratted supermarket opened. We just can't compete – half-price, sale-price, bonanza price, even no price.
Russ	Yes, but they're only doing that to get everybody in. Once they've been and realised how rubbish it is, they'll be straight back to us.
Rhona	No they won't, because we won't be here. We can't keep going at this rate. We're going to have to start cutting back and I'm afraid it's going to have to start...

Enter Shamus Leather and Paddy Shinebright; they come in all of a bustle, singing, dusting, they don't know about the news awaiting them – Russ and Rhona linger in the background trying to pluck up courage to let Paddy and Shamus know they won't be needed today

Shamus	Good morning to you Miss Hasbeen. *(singing)* Oh what a beautiful morning! Oh what a beautiful day!
Paddy	Good morning to you Mr Pout. *(singing)* I've got a wonderful feeling, everything's . . . *(they keep approaching the sack that has the spiders in, their attention keeps getting distracted)* Shall we give this sack of potatoes the once over for you, Miss Stringbean?
Rhona	Mr Leather . . .
Shamus	*(passes, before taking anything from the sack)* What'll be the matter with you? It's a fine day for a good . . .
Rhona	Just before you start . . .
Shamus	*(spots something on the floor at the other side of the shop)* Well, would you be looking at that. What some people drop these days. *(Picks up Ms Strategy's telephone and puts it in his pocket)*
Paddy	*(approaches the sack and picks it up to feel the weight)* Could do with a few extra in here, not that you seem to have been selling many that is . . .
Rhona	Exactly. That's just what I need to talk to you about. You see . . .
Paddy	Is there something bothering you?
Rhona	Well, you could put it like that. It's just . . . we're going to have to make you redundant.
Shamus	*(carries on – hasn't realised)* Read-what-was-that? I'm not that keen on books myself. Are you Paddy?
Rhona	No, you don't understand. We can't employ you any more.

They both keep approaching the sack and nearly going in there

Paddy	*(turns to Rhona)* You're looking a little bit tired, if I may say so. A good night's sleep, that's what you need.
Russ	In other words, you're sacked!
Shamus	Aye, we're trying to clean out the sacks. If you'll just . . .
Russ	You're fired. Got the boot. And here are your cards.

The message finally sinks in and Paddy and Shamus collapse in a heap with the shock

Rhona	We're ever so sorry, really we are. But since Insaneways opened, we just haven't had the customers. So we're going to have to let you go.
Russ	But we're sure this is just a temporary problem. We'll need you back – as soon as business picks up a bit.

Shamus and Paddy are in floods of tears – Russ and Rhona help to dry their eyes, pick up their belongings and leave the shop, just as the health inspectors enter

Rhona	If business picks up a bit.
Russ	Look on the bright side. Of course, things can only get better. *(there's a knock at the door)* I can feel it happening already. Our luck is just about to change.
Rhona	*(goes to the door, a foot comes straight inside and a hand offering proof of identification, Rhona takes it and reads it)*

	What's this? Health inspector?
Inspector 1	Good morning madam. *(all inspectors start walking around, picking up items, looking in sacks – but not the spider sack yet)*
Rhona	How can I help you?
Inspector 2	We have reason to believe . . .
Inspector 3	That your business . . .
Inspector 4	*(has a massive book of rules under arm, looks in book)* That is, Beansprout, Green and Regular . . .
Inspector 5	Has been breaking a few rules.
Inspector 4	*(looks in book)* Dear oh dear. We can't have that. Not rule breaking.
Inspector 1	In fact, we have had a tip off that . . .
Inspector 3	Your business . . .
Inspector 5	As registered under the 1962 green veg act . . .
Inspector 4	Here it is, 1962 in the rule book . . .
Inspector 2	Is contravening regulation 3.333 . . .
Inspector 4	Here it is . . . just a minute . . . I know it's here somewhere. This is the page. Regulation 3.333 – there we are in black and white. *(shows the book to Russ and Rhona and the audience)*
Inspector 1	The rule book quite clearly states . . .
Inspector 2	Very clearly . . .
Inspector 3	Without a shadow of a doubt . . .
Inspector 4	Look. *(taps the book)* You can read it here.
Inspector 5	That large, deadly spiders are not allowed in greengrocers.
Russ	Deadly spiders? *(jumps up on to a chair)* Where? I can't stand deadly spiders.
Rhona	Don't be silly, Russ. Whoever has tipped these gentlemen off doesn't know what they're talking about. *(to the inspectors)* I'm sorry, Inspectors. Whoever told you this is wasting your time. We are extremely careful not to break any of your rules.
Inspector 4	*(taps his nose – to the audience)* That's what they all say.
Russ	*(getting down off the chair)* Well, it's true.
Inspector 1	Then you won't mind if we have a good look around your premises.
Inspector 3	Will you?
Rhona	Please help yourselves. As you can see, we're not exactly overrun with customers at the moment.
Inspector 1	*(looks in the sack)* Aha! Pass the rule book.
Inspector 4	*(with obvious glee)* Why, you haven't found something have you?
Inspectors	Where? Where? Where?
Inspector 1	*(pulls out a large spider, Russ dives under the chair, shaking, inspectors rub their hands enthusiastically)* Well, well, well.
Inspectors	Well, well, well.
Inspector 4	This is definitely not allowed, according to regulation 3.333.
Inspector 1	I'm afraid to say . . .
Inspector 2	Ms Bean and . . .
Inspector 3	Mr Sprout . . .
Inspector 4	That this is a very serious offence . . .
Inspector 5	Indeed.
Inspector 1	We shall have to remove the evidence.
Russ	*(from under the chair)* Please do! And hurry!
Inspector 2	And give you a very hefty fine.
Rhona	I just don't understand how this can have happened. We are so careful . . .

Inspector 3	Not careful enough, if I may say so Ms Bean.
Rhona	Just how heavy will this fine be, exactly?
Inspectors	*(sharp intake of breath)* Very heavy.
Inspector 1	*(takes out his calculator, checks with inspector 4 and rule book)* Let's say . . . with VAT . . . fifty thousand pounds.
Bean&Sprout	Fifty thousand pounds? We can't afford that!
Inspector 2	That's not our problem.
Inspector 4	That's what happens if you break the rules in the rule book.
Inspector 1	We'll be sending the bill in the post. In the meantime, you'd better be a bit more careful in future.
Inspector 5	Much more careful.
Inspector 4	If you don't want us to throw the book at you, that is.

Inspectors exit

Rhona	That's it. We're doomed! How can we afford to pay fifty thousand pounds? We couldn't even pay Paddy and Shamus. Even worse, our reputation is ruined. Who will come to our shop now? *(approaches audience)* Would you buy fruit and veg from a shop with giant, hairy spiders in a sack of potatoes?
Russ	Even I have to admit things are looking a little . . . a little . . . bleak.

Song: Sing My Good Name

Rhona and Russ freeze – on come a very sad looking group of Bright Sides and Count Your Chickens

Chickens	We feel bad! We're in mourning Insaneways have got right up our nose Even Russ can see its dawning Poor old Beansprout'll have to close.
Brights	Oh no it won't.
Chickens	Oh yes it will. *(turn to audience to get them involved)*
Brights	Oh no it won't.
Chickens	Oh yes it will.
Bright 1	We're not going to let the evil lot at Insaneways close down our shop, are we?
Chicken 1	So how are we going to stop them?
Bright 2	We'll think of something!
Bright 3	We'll fight them in the cabbages!
Bright 4	We'll fight them in the turnips.
Bright 5	We'll fight them in the Brussels.
Brights	We will never surrender!

Enter Guardian Angel with weighing scales and shopping basket

Angel	Well, we'd better start doing something about it then.
Chicken 2	What have you got there?
Angel	This is my magic pair of weighing scales. We're going to mix together a few secret ingredients to make a little magic potion that's going to save the future of Beansprouts.
Chicken 3	Are you sure this is safe?
Chicken 4	*(puts on gas mask)* Tell me when it's over. I can't stand blood.

Angel	Oh, don't worry. It's not messy. One pound of watery mashed potatoes . . .

They pass the fruit and veg; each time Angel puts them in the weighing scales, and then transfers them to the basket where a Bright shakes it up

Chickens	Ugh!
Angel	One pound of worm-eaten stewed carrot.
Chickens	Ugh!
Angel	One pound of rotten lettuce scraped out of the fridge.
Chickens	Ugh!
Angel	Give it a good shake, repeat after me the magic spell . . . Shopping trolleys, aisles and baskets Insaneways are for the chop They might think they have us cornered Beansprout's where we're going to shop.

They all repeat the spell three times while grouped around in a circle; they cover over the basket, and on the last verse, move back to reveal Angel holding a large can of Chameleoni

Chickens	Is that it?
Chicken 5	Is that the master plan? A tin of pasta?
Angel	This is no ordinary pasta. This is Chameleoni. It's magic, you see.
Chicken 4	*(peering at can)* It doesn't look magic to me. It looks disgusting.
Angel	Taste it.
Chickens	Taste it?
Brights	Can we?

Angel spoonfeeds each of the Chickens and the Brights from the can – each, in turn, begins to smile

Angel	Well?
Bright 1	Delicious. Chocolate-mousse-and-double-cream flavour.
Chicken 1	Pretty tasty. Chips-and-brown-sauce flavour.
Bright 2	Out of this world . . . banana-and-peanut-butter flavour.
Chickens	Ugh!
Bright 2	Well, I like it!
Chickens	This can't be right. How come we've all tasted something different?
Angel	You haven't. It all came from the same can. Chameleoni tastes different to everyone who tries it. It becomes your favourite flavour, even banana-and-peanut-butter flavour . . . the minute you put this in your mouth, your taste buds get to work on it and change it into whatever they like most.
Bright 3	It's superb!
Bright 4	It's marvellous.
Bright 5	It's stupendous!
Chickens	That's not bad going.
Chicken 1	But how is it going to save the shop?
Angel	This isn't the only can. Have a look in the shopping basket. *(each of them go and collect a can from the basket)* We're going to put these on the shelves at Beansprouts, and every time a shopper

	buys them, a new one will take its place. Russ and Rhona will sell thousands and make a fortune.
Bright 1	Ingenious!
Bright 2	Amazing!
Bright 3	What wisdom.
Bright 4	What a brainwave.
Chicken 2	But I wish you'd learn us to use kilograms in your spells!

All exit, placing cans on the shelves of the shop; in the next scene, Beansprouts is filled with shoppers all clamouring to buy the cans from Russ and Rhona – the news reporter is there, as are the shoppers who were interviewed before

Reporter	*(to the audience)* And here we are at Beansprout, Green and Regular, to watch the extraordinary events that are happening here today. As you can see, there seems to be a little commotion over a brand new product on sale. Perhaps if I could ask this shopper . . .?
Shopper 6	*(waves walking stick around and pushes the reporter away)* Can't you see I'm busy, young man?

Reporter approaches someone else and taps them on the shoulder

Shopper 7	Just hold that for me a minute. *(passes him the basket while he or she waves his or her money in the air at Russ and Rhona)*
Reporter	Well, as you can see, there's a near riot going on here.

Enter four police officers

Police 1	Move along now, move along ladies and gentlemen. You're blocking the pavement.
Shopper 6	Leave me alone, young man. Young man, can't you see I'm busy, young man?
Police 2	Can't see what all the fuss is about myself.
Police 3	*(picks up a stray can and reads the label out loud)* Chameleoni – one taste and you're hooked. Hmm. *(puts his finger in to try some)* Ah! Blancmange and custard. Ah.
Police 4	*(does the same)* No . . . no . . . it's . . . ah. Tia Maria on the rocks!
Police 1	*(snatches the can)* No drinking on duty! *(tries it)* Why, that's not Tia Maria, it's . . . bread and dripping.
Police 3	We seem to have a little disagreement here. Perhaps we have some tasters in the audience who could settle this problem for us. *(approaches two or three in the audience to ask them what they think it tastes like)*
Police 1	What about these crowds then?
Police 2	I don't know about you, but I want some Chameleoni.

Police officers join the crowd who are beginning to chant

Crowd	Chameleoni! Chameleoni! That's what we want, what we want What we really, really want!

Shopper 1 emerges, carrying two heavy-looking carrier bags

Reporter	Excuse me. Haven't I seen you somewhere before? Didn't you used to shop at Insaneways?

Shopper 1	Insaneways? Never shop there. The bag handles always break. *(to the audience)* Anyway, they never paid me. *(exits)*
Shopper 2	Did you mention Insaneways? A real rip-off if you ask me. *(exits with carriers)*
Shopper 3	Rip it down. That's what they should do. Prices have gone up 600% since they thought Beansprouts were going out of business. *(exits)*
Shopper 4	And their staff always look so miserable. My Uncle Albert's sister had a friend who was sacked for wasting time showing a customer where the pickles were. *(exits)*
Shopper 5	And I'm sick of buying Insaneways deodorant, Insaneways bath foam, Insaneways shampoo. They all smell of dogs' droppings. *(exits)*
Shopper 6	Oh, it's you again, young man. Young man, don't you have anything better to do than holding up old age pensioners trying to do a little bit of shopping? *(gives him a whack with his walking stick and exits)*
Shopper 7	Who's got my basket? *(sees reporter who is still holding it and snatches it off him)* Thief!
Police	Thief? *(sees reporter)*
Police 1	Come along, sir. Let's be having you.
Police 2	Holding up all these decent, honest shoppers.
Police 3	You can help us with our enquiries back at the station.
Police 4	*(looks lovingly at the can of Chameleoni)* Anyone got a tin-opener?

They all exit, leading off the reporter

Reporter	Travis Dee reporting, and now onto the weather . . . *(voice trails away as he is led off)*

Rhona and Russ are the only ones still on stage

Rhona	I just can't believe it. Look at all this money we've made in just one day.
Russ	I told you, didn't I tell you things would get better? If things carry on at this rate, we'll be able to pay our fine, keep the shop open and invest a little in our own allotment.
Rhona	You know, Russ. I think you could be right. I think you could be right.

They exit; the next scene shows the managers sat in a meeting around a flipchart; enter Mr Sane and Master Ways

Mr Sane	Right boys! *(looks across at Ms Strategy and Mrs Monitor)* And girls. Give me those figures. Wow me with those statistics. Tell me, just once more, for the record, how well we're doing. Oh how I love these profit and profit meetings.

Managers look at each other worriedly, Master Ways gets out his Gameboy

Mr Sane	Put that away. Pay attention. For goodness sake. Take a little bit of pride in the family firm. Well . . . what are we waiting for? Come along Mr Margin. You first.
Mr Margin	*(stands up reluctantly and turns over the flip-chart to reveal a graph with descending line – he speaks very quietly behind his hand)* Well, we're . . . as you can see . . . we've made a little *(he*

	coughs at the same time he says the next word) loss this month.
Mr Sane	Speak up, man! I can't hear you.
Mr Margin	We've made a little *(coughs)* loss.
Mr Sane	We've made lots. All right, all right. But I want to know how much, not just lots. Of course we've made lots. But I need to know how much 'lots' is.
Ms Strategy	No, Mr Sane. It's not lots we've made this month, as you would see if you looked at the chart. We have actually lost money.
Mr Sane	*(stands up, looks confused, approaches flipchart, peers at it, turns his head, examines the chart again closely, and walks away)* Loss. As in deficit? In the red? In the brackets. No profit. No money, pauper, broke!
Ms Strategy	Something like that, sir.
Mr Sane	Mr Margin. This cannot be true. Tell me it's not true. *(shakes his head and looks at his feet)* Mrs Monitor. Mr Quality. Tell me this is some kind of nightmare.
Managers	It's true, sir, we're afraid to say The sales are looking grim The money is all going out With little coming in.
	We've checked the books, we've studied hard We've analysed these figures But business is not looking good The competition whipped us.
Mr Sane	What? What! Competition I hear you say? I can't believe . . . there is still competition? Put them out of business! What happened to our strategies? Ms Strategy – you're fired! What happened to our cheques? Mrs Monitor – you're sacked! What happened to our quality promise . . .?
Mr Quality	Well, er . . .
Mr Sane	Shut up! Get out of my sight! You're sacked, the lot of you.
Ms Strategy	Now look here –
Mr Sane	Out!
Mrs Monitor	I'm sure if we turned the graph the other way up …
Mr Sane	Out!
Ms Strategy	You'll regret this.

The managers exit

Master Ways	Can I go now?
Mr Sane	No! You're staying here. You'll have to look after the store. I've one or two c . . . c . . . competitors *(has difficulty saying the word)* to sort out. Whatever happens, Son, remember our little motto.
Master Ways	What's that Dad? Oh yes, I remember. An apple a day keeps the bank manager away.
Mr Sane	No, no! Not that one!
Master Ways	Too many solicitors cook the books?
Mr Sane	Come on, think. Think!
Master Ways	Don't count your invoices till they're in your account?
Mr Sane	I can't think what I sent you to that boarding school for . . .

When you're feeling hungry
When you want to scoff
Insaneways have the answer
We aim to . . . to . . .

Master Ways	Yes Dad?
Mr Sane	Dear oh dear. I seem to be having problems with my memorising. I think I'd better go and sit down somewhere. All this hiring and firing doesn't do me any good.

He is helped off by Master Ways; the managers return, led by Ms Strategy; they all look fed up apart from her, she is carrying a copy of the Yellow Pages

Mr Quality	What do we need a plumber for, Ms Strategy?
Ms Strategy	We don't need a plumber, fool!
Mrs Monitor	If you're looking for the job agency, it's left at the cross roads . . .
Ms Strategy	I certainly don't need another job.
Mr Quality	But if we've just been fired, it seems like a good idea.
Ms Strategy	That's not an idea. You wouldn't know an idea if it leapt out of your shopping basket shouting wholesale price!
Mr Margin	*(the most distressed)* I've really done it this time. Oh why, oh why didn't I lie?

The telephone goes; all the managers start running around looking for it

Managers	It's the phone. Who's phone? Which phone? Where phone? It's the phone. Who's phone? Which phone? Where phone?
Ms Strategy	*(very cool)* My phone. My new phone. Seem to have mislaid my old one. Hello? *(she speaks into her phone)* Yes, thank you for returning my call. I have a little job that needs doing.
Mrs Monitor	*(to other managers)* I told you she was after a plumber.
Managers	Shh.
Ms Strategy	He's just out of prison? Good. Good. I bet he is. Yes, it was dreadful. Fifteen years? That long, really? It is criminal these days, isn't it? No justice . . . and grievous bodily harm, such a little charge. Well, exactly. Did they ever recover the magnum? No? Well, at least that's something. So . . . to get back to business. We'll see him tonight. Around two am. Terms as we agreed? Good. Until then . . . and remember, don't breathe a word. I said don't breathe a word! *(puts phone away and addresses the managers)* It's all arranged for tonight.
Managers	All what's arranged?
Ms Strategy	With a little help from some of my contacts, we're going to do a little research of our own and a little re-distribution of goods.
Managers	What are you talking about?
Ms Strategy	Let me translate. At two o'clock in the morning, we're breaking into Beansprouts, nicking their Chameleoni and sticking our labels on to sell at Insaneways. Got it?
Managers	Why?
Ms Strategy	Dear, oh dear. I'm not getting very far, am I? Because . . . we want our jobs back and the only way we'll get our jobs back is by putting Insaneways back into the black, in the profit, sales going up. Got it?

Managers	Got it.
Mrs Monitor	There's just one problem. I can't make it tonight. A dinner party. You know how it is.
Mr Margin	I'll just check my diary. Oh dear. Would you look at this. I'm afraid I'm double-booked already. I'll have to take a rain check on this one. Sorry.
Mr Quality	What a nuisance. I'd promised to go and visit my mum this weekend, and I would so loved to have joined your little . . .little . . .
Ms Strategy	Hold it! No one is going anywhere. This is a top priority engagement. You'll all be there tonight or, Mr Margin, I'll be ringing up the *Shout and Echo*, and dropping a little bombshell about how a top local executive was once caught stealing lollipops from babies in the park. And, Mr Quality, I'm sure Mr Sane would be very interested to know why the petty cash has been disappearing more quickly than normal. As for you, Mrs Monitor, does Mr Sane know that you've been using his personalised Rolls Royce while he's on his yacht?
Managers	You wouldn't . . .?
Ms Strategy	Oh yes I would.
Managers	Oh no you wouldn't.
Ms Strategy	Oh yes I would. In fact, I think I'll make that phone call right now.
Managers	Okay. We'll be there.
Ms Strategy	*(to the audience)* So nice to have the support of your employees, don't you think?

They exit to return wearing long coats and gangster-type hats; they creep on following Ms Strategy, looking very nervous

Ms Strategy	*(whispering)* Don't be so nervous. You're making me nervous.

Carry on creeping along; from the other side of the stage, the burglars are creeping on as well – they don't see each other at first

Ms Strategy	*(to the audience)* You haven't seen Robin Snatchett, have you? He's supposed to be meeting us here. *(carries on creeping towards them)*
Robin	*(creeping with the burglars; to the audience)* You haven't seen that toffee-nosed Mrs Ratchy, have you? She's supposed to be meeting us here.

Robin and Ms Strategy bump into each other and both scream and put the boxes they are carrying in front of their faces; they timidly start to peer out, the Snatch and Drop gang switch on their torches

Robin	*(at the same time as Ms Strategy)* Oh, it's you!
Ms Strategy	*(at the same time as Robin)* Oh, it's you! *(fumbles for her torch)* Where's my torch gone?
Managers	*(notice the burglars have the managers' torches)* They're ours!
Ms Strategy	No we've wasted enough time. Let's get on with it. Put the cans in these boxes and let's get out of here as quick as we can. Time check.
Managers	*(look for their watches but they haven't got them; they start looking on the floor; meanwhile, the gang look at their watches and the managers peer over at them)* They're ours!

Robber 1	It's a fair cop!
Robber 2	Fair cop!
Robber 3	Fair cop!
Robber 4	Fair cop!

The gang and the managers creep into Beansprouts, take the cans off the shelves, and put them in their boxes – the phones go off

Managers	It's the phone. Who's phone? Which phone? Where phone? It's the phone. Who's phone? Which phone? Where phone?
Gang	Our phones. *(reach in their pockets)*
Managers	No they're not – they're our phones. Switch them off!
Robber 1	It's a fair cop!
Robber 2	Fair cop!
Robber 3	Fair cop!
Robber 4	Fair cop! *(they hand over the phones)*
Ms Strategy	Why do you keep saying 'fair cop'? It's getting on my nerves. Now, put the boxes over there and, just one more thing . . .

They transfer the boxes to Insaneways

Ms Strategy	Before you go, empty your pockets.

Managers go over and take purses, diaries, etc, from the gang

Gang	It's a . . .
Ms Strategy	Don't you dare!

Gang continue to exit, creeping around the edge of the stage, pause before they exit, turn around to the audience and hold up assorted goodies that they've managed to hold onto

Gang	Fair cop!

Exit gang

Ms Strategy	And now, with a little re-labelling, the Chameleoni is all ours. Insaneways is back on the map and, not only will we get our jobs back, but I think a little salary rise will be in order.

Managers exit rubbing their hands enthusiastically; enter the Chickens and the Brights, shaking their fists after the managers

Chickens	We feel angry! What a shame! They've got Chameleoni Will the shoppers at Insaneways Know that it is phoney?
Brights	Poor old Russ, but let's take heart We're sure to find a plan We've never let them beat us yet Though they've stolen every can.

Angel walks on with a can of Chameleoni and a magnifying glass

Chicken 1	What's that for?
Angel	Shh. I'm concentrating. *(peers closely at the can with the magnifying glass; appears to be reading something; all the Chickens and the Brights crowd around so that she can't see)* Aha! Just as I thought!
Others	*(to the audience)* Just as she thought?
Angel	They didn't read the small print.
Bright 1	Small print?
Angel	Right at the bottom of each can it says:

Chameleoni tastes divine
It's everybody's dream
But if it's stolen from its source
The taste becomes obscene.

Chicken 2	I don't understand.
Angel	The bad new for Ms Strategy and Insaneways is that stored on their shelves, in their proper place, Chameleoni tastes divine. But in the hands of thieves . . .
Brights	It tastes disgusting. Yuk! *(all imitate it tasting disgusting)*
Bright 3	Like Brussel sprouts?
Chicken 3	Like cold rice pudding?
Angel	No. Worse than that.
Others	Worse than that?
Bright 4	Semolina?
Chicken 4	Lumpy gravy?

Angel	Green and cold, wet and slimy
	Whatever is your worst
	The taste will linger on your tongue
	And cause a raging thirst.

Bright 5	I can't wait to see!

Exit from the stage; enter Ms Strategy surrounded by shoppers waving cans in the air

Shoppers	Give us our money! Give us our money!
Ms Strategy	I'm sorry, we don't give refunds. Company policy.
Shoppers	Give us our money! Give us our money!

Enter reporter

Reporter	Here we are, back at Insaneways. Where there seems to be a little disturbance.
Shoppers	Give us our money! Give us our money!
Shopper 8	This tastes disgusting.
Shopper 9	You've sold us rotten seaweed.
Shopper 10	I got a whole tin of maggot droppings.
Shopper 11	You were lucky. Mine was full of green-pea soup.
Shopper 12	Well, they sold me fish-flavoured meringue.
Shoppers	Give us our money! Give us our money!

Ms Strategy	*(starting to lose her temper)* I've told you. We don't give refunds and, in fact, *(looks at her watch)* is that the time? This store is about to close.

A trading standards officer enters, carrying an official clipboard

Officer	You're right there. The store is just about to close – for good.
Everyone	*(stops what they are doing and turn to face the officer)* For good?
Officer	I'm from Trading Standards. Who's in charge here?
Everyone	*(points to Ms Strategy)* She is!
Ms Strategy	*(starts backing away, shaking her head)* Oh no. I'm not in charge.

Mr Sane and Master Ways walk in

Ms Strategy	They're in charge. I've been sacked.
Mr Sane	What on Earth is going on here? *(to Ms Strategy)* What are you doing here? *(to Trading Standards)* Who are you?
Officer	Ah, Mr Sane?
Mr Sane	It is indeed. What seems to be the problem?
Shoppers	We want our money back! We want our money back!
Officer	Our department has been notified that Insaneways is breaking regulations 1, 3, 7, 44, 9, 28 . . . of the food and health act as well as contravening the patents law of 1854. So it is with great pleasure . . . I mean with great regret, that I have to inform you that your license to trade has been withdrawn. To put it bluntly, Mr Sane, you've had it.

Shoppers clap and cheer

Mr Sane	What? I . . . How . . . After all my years in the retail industry . . . This can't . . . You must be joking.
Officer	*(sticks a big sign on the door – 'Closed until further notice')* This is no joke. You're lucky we are not prosecuting. Actually, it might be an idea . . .
Reporter	Mr Sane. Can we have your reaction to this piece of news?
Mr Sane	Get out of here, the lot of you! Get out! Get out! Before I lose my . . . *(grabs smelling salts)* temper!
Reporter	Travis Dee reporting and now onto the weather . . .

Mr Sane grabs his microphone off him, everyone exits except Mr Sane and Master Ways

Mr Sane	*(into the microphone)* I'll have the lot of you! *(to the audience)* And you out there. I bet you're glad, aren't you? Well, you've not seen the last of me. *(shakes his fist)* You'll see.
Master Ways	Does that mean that we're not going to the match this afternoon, Dad?

Mr Sane boxes the boy's ears and drags him off; enter Paddy and Shamus

Paddy	Well, Shamus old son. This is the perfect site for our new business. I can see it now. Shinebright and Leather.
Shamus	Just a minute there, Paddy old son. Wouldn't you be meaning Leather and Shinebright?

Paddy	I would if that's what I was meaning, but seeing as it isn't, it's not.
Shamus	That'll be fine then. I'm glad we're agreeing. Because if we are going to be partners, we'll have to be agreeing about all sorts of things.
Paddy	Now would you look at that. Here come our new neighbours.

Enter Russ and Rhona

Paddy	And a good morning to you Ms Runnerbean and Mr Sprut. How's business these days?
Russ	Absolutely splendid, thank you Paddy. Couldn't be better. Marvellous. Since Insaneways has closed, business has just gone up and up.
Rhona	What he means is, we're doing quite nicely thank you, and if you'd like your jobs back . . .?
Shamus	Well that's very kind of you. But we're starting our own business now you know.
Paddy	That's right. A cleaning and laundry business. In fact, we'll be moving in right next door to you. Isn't that right, Shamus? Shinebright and Leather.
Shamus	That's right. Leather and Shinebright.
Rhona	Well, I'm pleased that things have worked out well for you.
Shamus	In fact, we're employing a few staff of our own now.
Paddy	Here they come. It's big business you know, these days, cleaning and laundering.

Enter the managers, Mr Sane and Master Ways, all dressed up in aprons, curlers and holding mops

Shamus	Hope you made a good job of **Leamwell Primary** [or whichever school]. They like their classrooms clean and tidy.
Ms Strategy	Cleaned from top to bottom it is.

Telephone goes

Managers	It's the phone. Who's phone? Which phone? Where phone? It's the phone. Who's phone? Which phone? Where phone?
Shamus	*(with Paddy)* Our phone!
Paddy	*(with Shamus)* Our phone!
Shamus	*(puts on a posh voice while answering the phone)* Hello. Leather and Shinebright. How can I be helping you? Yes, right, have they? No? Well, we'll soon put it right. I'm sorry about that. New they are, and not used to hard work if you ask me. Goodbye to you now. *(looks at managers)* That was **Mrs Montgomery** [or other such person at school] on the phone. Seems like the new cleaners have been sweeping stuff under the carpets. You'll all be getting the sack if you don't pull your socks up. *(to the audience)* Can't get the staff these days!
Paddy	Well, what are you waiting for? Back you go and make sure you do a proper job this time. Otherwise it'll be the sack for the lot of you.

Ms Strategy comes and looks at the phone

Ms Strategy	I'm sure I've seen that telephone somewhere before.

Shamus	*(embarrassed)* Phone? Which phone? Oh that phone. Couldn't be. Must be imagining things. Now off you go.

Managers exit, saying

Managers	We know we have been baddies We promise now we'll stop It seems a little harsh we think Our last word is 'fair cop'!
Bean/Sprout	Back to our greengrocers The queues are getting long We've beans to sell and sprouts to wash So here's our farewell song.

Enter Mr Sane carrying a tray with custard pies on it – he is selling the pies

Mr Sane	Custard pies! Custard pies! Get your home-made custard pies here! *(looks at and addresses audience)* What are you lot looking at? Told you I'd get back into business. After all, there's no keeping a good man down. It's thriving as well. Begin the panto season!
Panto dame	Two custard pies please, with plenty on top.
Mr Sane	With or without sauce?
Panto dame	As it comes, please.

Telephone starts to ring

Panto dame	Excuse me one moment. *(picks up phone and looks at Mr Sane)* Oh, he did, did he? He never! Put them out of business? Worms? Really? What a scoundrel. Of all the . . . I most certainly will. In fact, I'll be happy to. *(hangs up the phone and turns to the audience)* I hear this gentleman has been rather mean to a few people. Is that true? I hear he's been doing a little diddling, worm-planting, and other examples of atrocious behaviour. Is that true? Now, what I need to know is . . . *(holds up custard pie)* Should I? *(hopefully the audience will encourage the dame to throw a pie at Mr Sane)*

The disciples go shopping

Purpose: This play was used as part of a harvest assembly. It could only be used where a school had collected a sufficient display of produce, as it relies upon children being able to hand some over to the disciples.

Summary: The disciples have been sent out on a mission, to find five loaves and two fish with which to feed the five thousand. In a modern context, they do not find this task an easy one to accomplish. The fast-food restaurant is not accommodating, the supermarket has too many different types and is unsympathetic to their lack of money.

They try fishing for themselves, but do not realise that it is the school pond that they have ended up at, and this results in a catch they don't expect. At last they discover a school that is holding a harvest assembly and is prepared to donate some of their produce. But there is one important item they have forgotten.

Approximate running time: This is approximately 20 minutes in length.

Number of speaking parts: There are 19 speaking parts. All of them are relatively equally balanced, although the first disciples have perhaps the largest parts to play.

Number of potential parts: There are several ways in which this play could be opened up to a whole class. There could be additional people in the restaurant. In order to give them speaking parts, they could be ordering their meals before the disciples arrive. More children could be involved in feeding the goldfish and/or showing the disciples the range of food collected for the harvest festival.

Prop requirements: The main requirement is a good spread of produce for the harvest festival. A screen of some kind is needed so that the disciples can have their fishing lines suspended over the top, ready for the children to pull on. Done correctly, this is the most effective part of the play and the audience will love the tug of war and dialogue that goes with it. Fishing lines of some kind – these can be made quite easily out of canes and string – although, be warned, they do have a tendency of getting caught around each other.

A waitress outfit for the waitress and disciple-type clothing would be useful, but not essential.

Level of child intervention/adaptation: The children could make their own adaptations while showing the disciples the produce, and could even draw attention to some particular displays and donations.

Other comments and presentation: Careful thought has to go into where the produce is actually displayed. The stage has to remain largely free for the acting but, obviously, a selection of produce needs to be at hand for the children to draw attention to, and hand over to the disciples.

It is worth pointing out that not everyone is happy with updated versions of bible stories. You will know the approach taken by your school and whether such an adaptation is appropriate for your own context.

The disciples go shopping

Crowd scene inside the Queen's Diner

Waitress	Welcome to *Queen's Diner*. What can I get you? We've got chicken burgers with mayonnaise and relish, turkey burgers with onions and dips, double whammy whopper burgers, triple whale whammies with extra topping, fries, superfries and blockbuster fries with crinkle cut corners.
Disciple 1	I'd like some bread please.
Everyone	*(stop and stare)* Bread?
Waitress	I'm afraid we've got no bread. Just chicken burgers with mayonnaise and relish, turkey burgers with onions and dips, double whammy whopper burgers, triple whale whammies with extra topping, fries, superfries and blockbuster fries with crinkle cut corners. Now what would you like?
Disciple 1	No, it's bread I need. I've been sent to get five loaves of bread to feed five thousand, and they're all outside waiting, and they're very hungry.
Waitress	Don't they like burgers? We've got –
Disciple 1	Yes, I know what you've got. But I'm afraid it just won't do.
Waitress	Are you complaining?
Disciple 1	No, not complaining exactly. I just want some bread.
Waitress	If you have a complaint, we have an official complaints procedure. I'll just go and get the manager. *(exits)*
Disciple 1	*(shouting after her)* I don't want the manager. I want some bread!
Manager	*(enters)* I'm very sorry that *Queen's Diner* has not been able to satisfy your needs. We take customer satisfaction very seriously here. Just to show how sorry we are, our staff will provide you with a triple whale whammy on the house.
Disciple 1	*(getting annoyed)* I don't want a triple whale whammy! I want a loaf of bread and I don't care whether it's brown or white, or thin, medium or thick, or wholemeal or malted, or nutty or fruity. It can even be mouldy. But it's bread I need and bread I'll find. *(exits)*
Everyone	Well, there's no pleasing some people.

Scene clears to show disciples outside with others

Disciple 2	So what shall we do now?
Disciple 3	We've got to find some quick. Whatever will Jesus think if we can't even find one loaf of bread in a town like this?
Disciple 4	He doesn't realise how life has changed since his last sermons. It's just not so simple any more.
Disciple 5	What about trying that shop over there? Perhaps they have bread.
Disciple 6	It's worth a try.
Trolley man	Do you want a trolley?
Disciple 1	Actually, we were wondering if this was the sort of place we might be able to buy some bread?
Trolley man	Some bread? Are you serious?
Disciple 2	Here we go again!

Trolley man	Of course you can buy bread here. You can buy 125 types of bread. We even bake our own. And if you place an order, we can deliver up to five thousand loaves at a time.
Disciples	Now you're talking.
Disciple 3	How can we ever thank you? Perhaps if you would like to come to the sermon . . .?
Trolley man	Sorry folks, my shift doesn't finish until ten o'clock.

The disciples leave the trolley man and walk up and down the aisles

Disciple 1	*(shouting across)* Have you seen any yet?
Disciple 2	Have I seen any what?
Disciple 1	Bread of course!
Disciple 2	No bread here. Just pickled gherkins in spicy hot vinegar.
Disciple 1	Have you seen any yet?
Disciple 3	Any what?
Disciple 1	Bread of course!
Disciple 3	No bread here. Just Coco Pops and Rice Krispies.
Disciples	*(to disciple 1)* Well, have you seen any yet?
Disciple 1	Would I be asking you if I had?
Disciple 10	Stop!

All stop where they are

Disciple 10	I think I've found it!

The others all rush around

Disciple 1	Now which shall we have?
Disciple 2	How about a stick of French bread?
Disciple 6	No, too long.
Disciple 2	A cob loaf?
Disciple 8	Too nutty.
Disciple 2	Mighty White?
Disciple 9	Too chewy.
Disciples	*(to audience)* We just can't make our minds up!
Disciple 1	*(comes forward and picks out a member of the audience)* Which bread do you think should help to feed the five thousand people out there?

Disciples start to walk off stage with the bread

Detective	'Ello, 'ello, 'ello. What's going on here then? You can't do that.
Disciples	Do what?
Detective	Do that!
Disciples	Do what?
Detective	Take bread out of the supermarket without paying for it.
Disciple 5	But you've got more than you can possibly need, and it is for a very good cause.
Detective	Go on then, what is it this time? Aged grandparents? Homeless people? I've heard it all, you know. We always prosecute.
Disciple 6	It's Jesus. He's speaking to the people.
Disciple 7	Five thousand in total.
Disciple 11	And they're all rather hungry.
Detective	Well, that's a new one for me. Jesus, eh? I think the police

	might be rather interested in this. Sending twelve people to steal bread.
Disciple 1	It's just not like that. We weren't stealing it. We'd have returned it later. It's just we haven't much time and we've got to share it between the five thousand.
Detective	Sorry, I'm not with you. (holds up bread) This loaf of bread to feed five thousand people?
Disciple 2	That's right. Just a loaf of bread. Is that too much to ask?

Enter children from _____ school [fill in the gap]

Child 1	Did I hear you say you wanted some bread?
Disciples	Yes please!
Child 2	Come with us. It's our harvest festival today and we've got plenty of bread. The children have been very generous this year at their harvest festival. I'm sure we've got some to spare.
Disciples	At last! Someone who talks some sense.

Children lead disciples around the back of the stage and in from the other side

Disciple 1	You mean to say they've collected all this food together?
Disciple 2	And they're going to give it away?

Children nod

Disciples	We are impressed.
Child 1	We won't miss one loaf. And it's definitely in a good cause.
Disciple 1	Actually, we don't mean to be a nuisance, and we appreciate everything you've done. But it's actually five loaves we're needing to feed five thousand.
Child 2	Five? All the better. (gets the loaves) And don't forget, if you need anything else, just ask!

Exit disciples behind screen and children; fishing lines appear over the top of the screen

Disciple 1	(off stage) Have you got a bite yet?
Disciple 2	(off stage) Not even a nibble.
Disciple 3	(off stage) We've been here an hour already. Everyone will have gone home by the time we catch anything.
Disciple 4	(off stage) Did you hear him ask for two fish as well as five loaves?
Disciple 1	Look, it's no good complaining now. We know what we've to do and if we carry on making all this fuss, we'll never catch anything.
Disciple 5	(off stage) Couldn't they manage with the bread?
Disciples	(off stage) No!

Three children enter in wellington boots

Child 1	I'm glad it's our turn to feed the goldfish.
Child 2	Any excuse to get out of the maths lesson!
Child 1	Look at all those fish! What a life! They never have to sit through mental maths do they?
Child 2	Look at that one. It's enormous. Twice as big as my goldfish at

	home.
Child 3	Just look at all this rubbish. *(bends over and starts picking items up – gets hold of one of the lines)* Hang on a minute, what's this?
Child 1	Looks like a fishing line to me.
Child 2	Don't be silly. Who'd go fishing for goldfish in a school pond?
Child 3	I don't know. But I'm going to find out! *(starts pulling on the line – from behind the screen there comes a shout)*
Disciple 1	I've got one! I've got a bite! At last! It's a strong one though. Hold this while I reel it in!
Child 1	Oh no you don't, you goldfish-napper!
Disciple 2	It can talk! Your fish can talk! Don't let go!
Disciple 1	I can't hold it much longer! It must be enormous. It's slipping! *(child falls backwards)*
Disciples	You lost it.

Disciples emerge from behind screen

Disciple 2	The only bite we'd had and you lost it.

Disciples and children come face to face

All	It's you!
Child 1	I thought you'd got everything you needed!
Disciple 6	No. It turns out we needed two fish as well as five loaves.
Disciple 5	So when we saw this water, we thought we could catch some fish here.
Child 2	But these are our school's goldfish. You can't have these!
Disciple 4	We didn't know they belonged to you.
Disciple 3	We're really sorry.
Child 3	I'm afraid we can't help you out with this one either. Fish is not part of our harvest collection.
Child 4	It was difficult enough collecting fresh cakes, let alone fresh fish. Imagine the pong?
All	Yuk!
Child 1	Perhaps not *fresh* fish . . . but I've got an idea.

Exit stage together and come around other side

Child 1	Look, we've got tins of mackerel, tins of sardines, tins of tuna.
Disciple 1	That's all fish. I'm sure that would do.
Child 2	Here you are. Take three, just to be on the safe side.
Disciple 3	No, that's no good. Then it would be feeding the five thousand with five loaves and three fish. We can't change the story.
Disciples	How can we ever thank you?
Child 3	Now, you're sure there's nothing else you need?
Disciples	Sure!
Children	Absolutely sure?
Disciples	Positive.
Children	Very positive, or just a little?
Disciples	Very.

All shake hands – disciples exit; children sit on the edge of the stage

Child 1	Fancy meeting the disciples!

Child 2	No one would ever believe us.
Child 3	*(to audience)* You believe us, don't you?
Child 4	Do you think we'll ever see them again?
Child 1	I doubt it. Five loaves, two fish. There was nothing else.

Disciples return from the back

Disciple 1	Um . . . you don't happen to have a tin-opener, do you?
Children	*(shake heads)* Ugh!

The golden goose

Purpose: This is a traditional story retold in script form, with some more contemporary illustrations to the theme. The story it is based on is an excellent example of a traditional fairy story with many key elements. The three brothers, a king who sets the challenge for someone to win the heart of the princess, the youngest brother showing the best spirit, the wise old man who is rebuffed by the older brothers, the good turn resulting in success with the challenge. The story and play can be used to highlight these traditions of story writing. It is ideal for a slightly longer assembly, which emphasises the moral of being kind, even when we can't necessarily expect anything back in return.

Summary: Based on the traditional story, *The golden goose*, the youngest son of a woodcutter is sent out to chop wood after his two elder brothers are unsuccessful in their attempts. The youngest son behaves civilly to an old man, whereas his brothers were both rude to him. As a reward, the son is directed towards a tree where he discovers a golden goose. During his journey through town and country, he discovers that everyone who touches the goose becomes stuck to it. The resulting chaos is sufficient to make a particularly sombre princess laugh, and so he wins her hand in marriage.

Approximate running time: This is a slightly longer play of between 15 and 20 minutes.

Number of speaking parts: There are nine major parts that take the majority of the script. There are ten additional minor parts with one or two lines only.

Number of potential parts: This play could quite easily be built into a whole class assembly as the youngest son can pick up more characters who become stuck to the goose. It would be quite easy to give them an additional line each to say as they become hooked.

Prop requirements: Some kind of prop to act as a goose is particularly useful for this. We actually used a cuddly duck, but any soft toy that bears some resemblance to a bird would probably do. Other useful items include clothes for the king and princess, a basket for the food given to the brothers, an axe, and a bandage for their injuries. A foam dumbbell is useful at the beginning, or an imitation one could quite easily be made.

Level of child intervention/adaptation: At the beginning when the jester and contortionist are trying to make the princess laugh, there is opportunity for children not only to supply their own jokes, but also for other talents and party pieces to be used. 'How would you make the princess laugh?' can become several drama lessons on its own. When the second eldest brother is looking for a tree to chop down, children can be encouraged to improvise in their involvement with the audience and extend this section.

The golden goose

Jester	*(children choose some of their favourite jokes for the jester to make as the princess looks on completely unimpressed)*
Princess	Heard it! That was on telly last night. Can't you do better than that?
King	Haven't you made her laugh yet? Soldiers, take him away.

Jester is escorted off and we hear a scream from behind the screen

Princess	Father, do you have to have everybody beheaded who can't make me laugh? It's getting to be a bit of a bore! *(yawns)*
King	I tell you, daughter, no-one is going to marry a princess who never smiles, and I can't keep on spending all my money on your fancy clothes. It's time you made your own way in the world. Next!

Enter a contortionist, pulling funny faces

Royals	Next!
Contortionist	You want another one?
Royals	No! Get him off!
Soldier	With pleasure, your majesties.

As before, but this time from behind the screen the soldier starts to laugh

King	Get on with it!
Soldier	I can't. He's so funny.
Princess	It looks like we'll just have to do it ourselves.

King and princess move behind a screen; there is a scream, and they all exit; three brothers enter, carrying a dumbbell

Brother 1	Look at this, Bruv. I can do eight curls with my eyes closed.
Brother 2	That's nothing. I can do eighteen curls with my eyes closed and one hand on my head tickling my left ear. Watch!
Brother 1	Right, Dummling. How many curls can you do? *(passes the third brother the dumbbell and Dummling drops it; the other two brothers laugh)*
Brother 2	You're a wimp!
Brother 1	I think he's more of a chimp, actually! *(runs around making chimp noises)*

Their parents enter, their father carrying an axe

Dummling	Dad. They're making fun of me again. Stop them will you, Dad?
Dad	Typical. Didn't I tell you that you should be out chopping wood? *(passes axe to brother 1)* The fire's nearly gone out. You'd better get some wood quickly from the forest or we'll all freeze to death. Now scoot!
Mum	Take this with you. One of my finest pancakes and a bottle of wine. It'll keep you going.

Dummling, brother 2 and parents exit; brother 1 is in a forest where there is an old man

Brother 1	*(hiccuping)* Perhaps I shouldn't have drunk so much at once. I can't see the trees, never mind chop them down.
Old man	Then perhaps you might like to share the rest with me? A little of your pancake would be pretty welcome too.
Brother 1	Who are you? You've got a cheek. Be off with you before I mistake you for a tree. *(lifts the axe above his head and pretends to chop him; the man runs off)* Of all the nerve. Hic! Now, where was that tree? *(falling around, swings the axe, and brings it round so sharply, he cuts his own arm instead)* Ow! Help! Mummy! *(runs off stage)*

Back at home, brother 1 is in tears; Mum wraps a bandage round and round his arm

Dad	But we still haven't any wood and I'm freezing! *(he hands the axe to brother 2)* Your turn, and I hope you do better than your useless brother.
Mum	Here's your wine and pancake, but don't drink it all at once!

Brother exits, and family exit, then scene changes to show him walking around the forest where there is an old man

Brother 2	*(drinking while walking and hiccuping)* That can't have been a full bottle. I bet that Dummling brother of mine had a drink first. Now, I'm sure there were some trees around here somewhere. *(grabs hold of a member of the audience)* Is this a tree ready for chopping?
Old man	Share your pancake with me and I'll show you a good tree to chop.
Brother 2	Do you think I'm mad? I'm not sharing my mum's delicious pancakes. You can make some of your own! Ah, I think I can see one here! *(takes a swipe, misses and cuts his leg instead, starts hopping around)* It attacked me! *(runs home, old man exits)*

Back at home, brother 2 is in tears; Mum wraps a bandage round and round his leg

Dad	We still haven't any firewood. I suppose we'll all freeze to death.
Dummling	Don't worry. I'll go and get some.
Others	You?
Dummling	Yes, me!
Brothers	But you're Dummling. You never do anything right.
Dad	I bet you can't even lift this axe! *(hands the axe over to Dummling)*
Dummling	*(dropping the axe)* I don't suppose you've got a lighter one, have you?
Mum	Now come on, all of you. Give him a try. We've nothing to lose. I'm afraid there isn't any wine left and I've run out of pancake mix. But I've got some ash-baked cake and a bottle of sour beer.

Dummling sets off to the forest where there is an old man

Dummling	*(to audience)* Ash baked cake – yuk! Sour beer – disgusting!
Old man	Are you saying I'm disgusting?
Dummling	I'm sorry, I didn't see you there.

Old man	That's all right. You don't happen to have anything to eat and drink do you?
Dummling	Here. You're welcome to share it. *(passes the bag over)*
Old man	How tasty – pancake! How delicious – wine!
Dummling	Pancake? Wine? Well I never.
Old man	Seeing as you've been so kind, take a tip from an old man. There's a tree over there. Chop it down and you'll find something at its roots. *(exits)*

Dummling walks across to where he is pointing and chops; then he picks up a golden goose

Dummling	A goose with golden feathers. Wow! Forget the firewood. We can get central heating with this. *(begins to walk around the hall and picks up people as he goes, starting in a tavern)*
Girl 1	What a lovely golden goose. *(to the audience)* While he's not looking, I'll have this for myself. *(points up to the sky)* What's up there, Dummling? *(he looks up and the girl tries to grab it but her hand sticks)* Hey, what have you done to it? I can't get my hand free!
Girl 2	What's the matter? *(sees the goose)* Ooh, I wouldn't mind one of those myself. Hey you two, have you seen that funny looking bird? *(tries to grab the goose but is held fast)* Hey, what's happened? I'm stuck!
Girl 3	Well I never. I'd like . . .
Girls 1 & 2	No! *(girl 3 gets hold)* Too late!
Dummling	Well, you'll just have to come home with me!
Girls	Let us go!
Landlord	What are you doing? Leave my daughters alone. *(grabs hold of one)* I'm stuck! Help!
Farmer	Hey landlord. I want some pie and peas. Don't be running off after your daughters. Come back! *(grabs hold and gets stuck)* Hey, let me go!

A woodcutter walks by with an axe

All	Can you get us free? We're stuck!
Woodcutter	*(raises axe and grabs hold of farmer's arm)* What's happened? I'm stuck too!

A carpenter walks by with a saw

All	Can you get us free?
Carpenter	*(gets saw at the ready and gets hold of woodcutter's arm)* What's happened? I'm stuck too!

The whole procession arrives in front of the palace; Dummling stops suddenly and they all fall on top of each other; they take it in turns to shout out

All	Let me go!

Princess comes to see, looks hard and walks around

Princess	Well I never. What a set of idiots. In fact you look . . . you

	look . . . *(starts to crack up)* really, really funny. *(collapses laughing)*
King	*(starts to walk up to them to shake Dummling's hand)* Let me congratulate you. You are now my future son-in-law. You will marry the princess.
All	No don't! Don't touch him!

As the king reaches to shake his hand, all the others are set free and drop on to the floor

Dummling	*(turns to the audience)* See, I'm not such a wimp after all!

Mystic Joseph

Purpose: This play takes a familiar bible story and sets it in a contemporary context. It is particularly appropriate for use around harvest time and can lead to an examination of the actual bible story. Children could be encouraged to write scripts of their own for other parts of the Joseph story. It could be used as part of a harvest celebration, or stand on its own during an assembly.

Summary: This is a play based upon Joseph's accurate dream interpretations and his subsequent release from prison to interpret Pharaoh's dreams. The characters are transposed into a more modern setting, which is designed to show the relevance of its main themes to modern life. The play concludes when Joseph is asked to manage the storage of food during the years of plenty. The audience is encouraged to read the rest of the story for themselves.

Approximate running time: This is a short play of about 10 minutes duration.

Number of speaking parts: There are ten separate speaking parts and a chorus.

Number of potential parts: It is up to you how many children the chorus consists of. You may choose to give some children individual lines or lines to say in a pair.

Prop requirements: One or two props are desirable for this. A bible, an axe, a bottle of wine. Two benches for the beds of the prisoners are useful, and appropriately smart clothes for the prime minister and politicians.

Level of child intervention/adaptation: Children can be encouraged to extend the play into the next stage of events using the same setting. How would they translate the sequel, and also the prequel to this section? Some of the phrases and references will become dated. There will always be up-to-date alternatives, which should replace the originals.

Other comments on presentation: The play opens up the opportunity to discuss the relevance of bible stories to the present. How might they update other stories? What parallels can they see between the stories and other plays and stories they have come across? Other relevant discussions include the relevance of dreams and people's interpretations.

Mystic Joseph

Scene one

Two children are on stage; one is reading the bible

Child 1	What are you reading?
Child 2	The bible.
Child 1	The what?
Child 2	The bible.
Child 1	You're joking. What do you want to read that for? It's old-fashioned. It's all about men in long dresses with long hair and beards.
Child 2	No it's not. There are some really brilliant stories and you can learn a lot from them.
Child 1	Oh yeah?
Child 2	Yeah.
Child 1	Oh yeah?
Child 2	Yeah!
Child 1	Right, show me!
Child 2	Okay. You remember the story of Joseph and his brothers?
Child 1	The one with the long coat?
Child 2	The one where Joseph makes his brothers jealous . . .
Child 1	Yeah! My brothers are always getting more pocket money than me . . . and then they sell him as a slave . . .
Child 1	Now there's a thought. I wonder how much I could get for mine?
Child 2	You see, it's a good story isn't it? Well, it's like real life . . . well, like my brothers anyway.
Child 1	But what about all the other bits? The wine servers and pharaohs, and cows on the banks of the River Nile. That's not like real life.
Child 2	Of course it is. Look, it doesn't have to be a wine server, or a cow. It could just as easily be . . .
Child 1	Yes?
Child 2	It could be . . .
Child 1	Come on then.
Child 2	Look. I'll show you.

Enter three prisoners; they lie down on benches

Butler	*(groans and pretends to be asleep, sits bolt upright as though talking in his or her sleep)* I'm so sorry, Prime Minister. I didn't mean to spill red wine all over the queen's new dress. Please don't sack me.
Baker	*(also pretends to be asleep, sits bolt upright as though talking in his or her sleep)* I'm so sorry, Prime Minister. I didn't mean to serve stale bread to the American president. It wasn't my fault his fillings came out after all. Please don't sack me.
Joseph	*(sleeping between the two, sits upright and speaks to the audience)* Can't a man get any sleep around here? It's like this all the time. These two need locking up.
Butler/Baker	*(wake up)* But Joseph, we are locked up!

Butler	And until the prime minister forgives us, we've just got to make the best of it we can.
Baker	Trouble is, I keep having these terrible dreams. You'll never guess what I dreamt last night.
Butler	You met the **Spice Girls**? [or some other topical band]
Baker	Try again.
Butler	You played football at Wembley?
Baker	You must be joking!
Butler	What then?
Joseph	*(has been trying to sleep, but sits up again)* Will you just get on with it. I'm trying to get some sleep here.
Baker	I dreamt that I was in Tesco with three loaves of bread in my trolley, when a whole load of shelf-stackers came and emptied the trolley and put it all back on the shelves.
Butler	I bet you couldn't pay for it, could you?
Baker	'Course I could, clever clogs. So, what have you been dreaming about lately?
Butler	I don't know if I should tell you. You'll only laugh.
Baker	Go on. Promise I won't. I told you mine.
Butler	All right then. I suppose it won't do any harm. It's strange really, because it's a bit like yours in a way.
Baker	Copycat.
Butler	I said you'd take the mickey.
Baker	I'm sorry. Carry on. I won't say anything else. Promise.
Butler	I dreamt that in my trolley there were three bottles of red wine, and the prime minister sent his stretch limousine to pick me up from outside Morrisons.
Baker	In your dreams!
Butler	Exactly. But what do you think it means?
Baker	Probably that you've got a very big head and need it examining.

During the play there is a chorus

Chorus	Tut, tut. You're off again You never will agree Perhaps if you knew what they meant The boss would set you free.
Baker/Butler	Tell us what the dreams mean then!
Chorus	How should we know?
Joseph	*(sits up and starts to take part again)* I know.
Chorus	Oh no you don't.
Joseph	Oh yes I do.
Chorus	Oh no you don't!
Joseph	Oh yes I do!
Chorus	Go on then, tell us.
Joseph	Butler.
Butler	Yes?
Joseph	In three days the prime minister will give the courts evidence of your innocence and you will be released.
Butler	I'm free?
Joseph	I said, in three days.
Butler	Oh. *(looks dejected)*
Baker	And what about me?

Joseph	In three days, the prime minister will order . . . *(mimes chopping off his head)*
Baker	Not . . . *(repeats mime)*
Joseph	I'm afraid so.

| Chorus | Now, now. Is it really true
You wouldn't pull our leg?
This boy is in the running
For replacing Mystic Meg. |

Prime minister enters; he or she shakes the butler's hand and hands him a bottle of wine and a tea towel; the baker's knees start shaking; the prime minister returns and makes chopping actions; he leads the baker off stage with his knees knocking; from the back of the stage an axe is raised and off stage there is a scream

Scene two

The prime minister is lying down, sleeping, and sits bolt upright

PM	Help! Help! They're coming for me.
Servant	*(runs on)* Who's coming for you?
PM	The sausage rolls! The sausage rolls and the pickled onions. They're going to eat me up just like they ate up the other ones.
Servant	*(to the audience)* He really has been working too hard.
PM	It's my dream. I dreamt that seven fat sausage rolls were eaten by seven thin sausage rolls, and then seven tiny pickled onions ate up seven really big pickled onions. What can it mean?
Servant	Um . . . It's time you had a holiday?
PM	Look, bring me the best politicians in the land. Let them work out what my dreams mean.
Servant	You'll be lucky.

Enter three politicians

MP 1	Well, Prime Minister. I think it means I should have a 70% pay rise.
Chorus	Rubbish!
MP 2	Well, Prime Minister. I think it means you should throw seven parties for your best politicians.
Chorus	Rubbish!
MP 3	Well, Prime Minister. I think it means you should have a seven-year break.
Chorus	Rubbish!
Butler	What about Joseph? He'll know.

| Chorus | Mystic Joseph, with God's help
Is a dream translator
He sorted out the butler's dream
And now he's your best waiter. |

Joseph is brought on by two guards who are telling him about the dreams under their breath

| Joseph | Pickled onions? Really? Sausages? Never! |

PM	Well?
Joseph	Yes?
PM	What does it mean?
Joseph	*(to audience)* I really ought to start charging for this. It means, Prime Minister, that there will be seven years of plenty. The supermarkets will be full to overflowing, tins of beans will roll off the shelves, and the school canteens will be packed solid with chips. But then . . .
Chorus	Then?
PM	Then?
Butler	Then?
Guards	Then?
Joseph	Nothing.
Chorus	Nothing?
Joseph	Nothing. There will be seven years when there won't be enough to go around. The shelves will be empty and children will queue for the last spoonful of mashed potato, and the last soggy Brussel sprout.

The prime minister starts to panic

Everyone	Don't panic!
PM	I'm not panicking. Prime ministers never panic.
Joseph	All we have to do . . .
PM	Yes?
Joseph	All we have to do is to save as many tins of beans and packets of chips as we can when there's plenty, and eat them when there's none.
PM	Oh, simple. And who's going to do all this?
Joseph	I'll do it!
PM	Now why didn't I think of that?

A pause – while everyone raises their eyebrows – as if everyone knows exactly why he didn't

Chorus	Three cheers for Joseph Hip, hip hooray . . . He's our hero, he'll store our food And make sure we're all fed No longer locked up in the clink He's our main man instead.

Exit characters, return to initial children

Child 2	Well? What did you think? A good story, isn't it?
Child 1	Not bad, I suppose. Just out of interest, not that I'm too bothered or anything, but . . . what happened next?
Child 2	I thought you said you weren't bothered?
Child 1	I'm not. But did he do it? Did Joseph store up all the food and stop the people from starving?
Child 2	He certainly did. In fact, he did much more than that. He found his brothers again.
Child 1	And?
Child 2	And what?
Child 1	What happened?

Child 2   Well then . . . wait a minute. I'm not giving everything away.
Look, it's here in the bible. Read if for yourself instead!

So you think you're going home tonight?

Purpose: This play can be used as part of a discussion about dealing with crises and emergencies. It could also be used as a more light-hearted approach to examining some of the issues linked to Anne Frank's period of forced internment and the implications of evacuation. Its short length and fast pace make it ideal for a drama group assembly.

Summary: A group of children are prevented from leaving the school at their usual time. They soon discover how uncomfortable life can become if separated from their routine, possessions and the people they love. Finally, they receive the good news that the hazard preventing their release is removed. Make way for the rush!

Approximate running time: 10 minutes but additional sections could be added and the period of confinement could be increased.

Number of speaking parts: The teacher is the main character with the other 12 children's parts largely being equivalent. Child 6 has a slightly greater role to play as he or she is walking on and off stage, providing the link between the outside world and the classroom.

Number of potential parts: You could include a number of other children to make up the class and give them each an additional line in each section. Too many, however, and the pace would be slowed down to the point where it becomes tedious. Probably a maximum of 20 could be considered.

Prop requirements: There are very few essential props. Most essential are the pyjamas that the children hold up. Each child can be asked to contribute to this collection – it causes quite a lot of amusement, especially if they can be encouraged to hold up each other's. A tray for Child 6 is useful, although having too many additional objects to balance makes it fraught with retakes. A mortarboard and gown or other way of indicating the teacher is useful, but not essential.

Level of child intervention/adaptation: Children could alter the script using some of their own preferences for activities they have to be home for, and drinks they prefer. Additional sketches could be included with other essential but inadequate items being brought in.

Other comments on presentation: If you feel adventurous and want your play to go out with a bang, you can hire or create a gorilla suit for someone to appear in right at the end, when all the characters have exited. He or she could make some remark such as "Where has everyone gone?" to the audience.

So you think you're going home tonight?

Children are sitting in class watching the teacher

Teacher	And in which country was Anne Frank born?

Knock on the door; child runs in with a note for the teacher, who reads it

Teacher	*(to the child)* Are you sure?
Child 6	Mr Blatcher gave me the note himself.
Teacher	Well, thank you. *(child exits)* As I was saying . . . in which country was Anne Frank born?

Hands go up; bell rings; children stand up ready to go

Teacher	Sit down.
Child 1	But Sir, [or Miss] the bell's gone. It's home time.
Teacher	No it's not.
Child 2	Yes it is, Sir. Look, it's three-thirty.
Teacher	So it is.
Child 3	Three-thirty is home time.
Teacher	So it is.
Child 4	So, we're going home.
Teacher	No you're not.
Children	Oh yes we are!
Teacher	Oh no you're not.
Children	Why not?
Teacher	Because I've just received a note from Mr Blatcher to say that a wild and dangerous gorilla has just escaped from Securiless Zoo, and nobody is allowed to leave the building until further notice.
Children	Oh Sir!
Teacher	Don't blame me.
Child 1	But I'm hungry.
Child 2	I've got my piano lesson at four o'clock.
Child 3	I want to watch Grimshaw High.
Child 4	I've got my rabbit to feed.
Child 5	I've got me to feed!
Teacher	I'm sure they won't let us starve. They'll send us some food. There's nothing to worry about. Now, let's make ourselves comfortable, and it'll probably be along in a minute.

Knock at the door

Teacher	What did I tell you?
Children	Who's there?
Child 6	A child with a tray.
Children	Come in but watch the step!

Child enters and stumbles

Children	We told you to watch the step.
Child 7	Is this all?

Child 8	Where's the rest?
Child 9	My mummy says I can only eat brown bread.
Child 10	What is it?
Child 6	Tuna paste sandwiches.
Children	Tuna paste sandwiches? Yuk!
Child 9	My mummy says I'm allergic to tuna paste.
Child 6	Take it or leave it. That's all the helicopter dropped us. *(exits)*
Child 11	I'll have it then. I like tuna.
Child 12	You like anything.
Child 11	That's not true. I don't like . . . I don't like . . . well, I'm not very keen on lumpy rice pudding. When it's cold that is, and the rice isn't cooked properly.
Child 12	*(to the audience)* See what I mean?
Teacher	Well, if there isn't anything else to eat, I suppose we'd better try them.

All take a sandwich, take a bite together facing the front, and pretend to choke

Children	We need a drink!

Knock at the door

Children	Who's there?
Child 6	Child with a drink.
Children	Come in but watch the step.

Child enters and stumbles

Children	We told you to watch the step!
Child 7	Is this all?
Child 8	Where's the rest?
Child 10	What is it?
Child 6	Water.
Children	Water? Yuk!
Child 9	My mummy said I can only drink Perrier water.
Child 6	Take it or leave it. That's all the helicopter dropped us.
Child 11	Well, I suppose it could be worse.
Child 12	*(takes a drink)* No it couldn't!
Child 4	Where's my glass?
Child 6	I'm afraid they only dropped the bottles. You'll just have to share!
Child 9	My mummy says I'm not to drink from bottles.
Teacher	I think we might just have to make the best of it. Anyone for water?
Child 12	We could always pretend it was something else. *(turns to child 2)* What's yours going to be?
Child 2	Ice cold, diet cola. *(bottle is passed around)*
Child 3	Mine is freshly squeezed orange juice.
Child 4	Mine's Ribena.
Child 5	Mine's . . . mine's . . . empty!
Child 6	Well, I'm afraid you'll just have to wait until they drop us breakfast. *(exits)*
Children	Breakfast?
Child 7	I'm not staying here all night!
Child 9	I want my mummy!

Child 10	I want my pyjamas!
Child 3	I want my hot cocoa and dunking biscuit.
Child 8	I want my Noo-noo.
Children	Your what?
Child 8	Well . . . it's a blanket really. But I've had it since I was little.
Children	Ahh.

Knock at the door

Children	Who's there?
Child 6	Child with pyjamas.
Children	Come in but watch the step!

Child enters and stumbles

Children	We told you to watch the step.
Child 7	Is this it? I thought you said you'd brought our pyjamas.
Child 8	You've forgotten to bring mine.
Child 10	I can't find mine either.
Child 6	I said that I'd brought some pyjamas, not that I'd brought yours.
Children	Other people's pyjamas? Yuk!
Child 9	My mummy says you can get fleas from wearing other people's clothes.
Child 6	Take it or leave it. That's all the helicopter dropped us. *(exits)*
Child 11	Well, actually, I wouldn't mind trying these on. A bit big perhaps, but . . .
Child 12	*(holds up stripy pair)* Do you think these would suit me?

Children dive in and take a pair each – child 9 is left with a totally inappropriate pair or nightie

Child 9	I can't wear these!
Children	Because your mummy says . . .
Child 9	*(starts to cry)* I want my mummy!
Child 1	I want my mummy.
Child 7	I want my mummy.
Teacher	I want my mummy too!
Child 5	I want my daddy.
Children	We want to go home.

Knock at the door

Children	Who's there?
Child 6	Child with some good news.
Children	Come in but watch the step!

Child enters but doesn't stumble

Children	You remembered the step!
Child 7	What's the news then?
Child 8	Have they dropped us some pizza?
Child 9	Have you found some glasses?
Child 11	I know, you've brought my Noo-noo.

Child 6	Even better. They've caught the gorilla and you can all go home for your supper.
Children	Yes! *(cheer)*
Child 11	Oh, I was quite looking forward to wearing those pyjamas . . . perhaps if no-one minds . . .
Child 3	Right, let's get out of here!
Children	*(clamour)* Me first . . . me first . . .
Teacher	Hold it! Act your age, everybody. Everyone's going home. There's no panic. Just take your turn . . . but it's me first!

Teacher runs out followed by all the children

Promise you won't look

Purpose: This is a short play with a limited number of parts that is suitable for a group to perform. It is relatively straightforward to prepare and produce, relying on a limited number of plots. It has been used as part of an assembly that emphasised the power of temptation and the acceptance of how difficult it can be to resist when we are exhorted not to do something.

Summary: This is a series of short sketches, all based on being tempted to look at something, or do something we shouldn't. The sketches are linked by one of the main characters leaving a prop for the next sketch.

In the first scene, a child and father can't resist opening a box to discover it belongs to a superhero. In the second, Adam and Eve can't resist the apple. In the third, Bluebeard's wife can't help looking in the locked room. In the final sketch, the Large family can't resist testing Granny's cake.

Approximate running time: This is a short play of about 10 minutes duration.

Number of speaking parts: There are 12 main parts, all relatively equally balanced.

Number of potential parts: More sketches around the same theme could be added, e.g. *Pandora's box*.

Prop requirements: The play does benefit from a small number of key props. These include a box with a superhero outfit included, an apple and a cake. I used a real cake during the actual performance, and the children thoroughly enjoyed having a share of it as their reward at the end.

Level of child intervention/adaptation: Children may have their own ideas for additional sketches that could be included. There are many examples from myths and stories around the world of characters who couldn't resist looking back, or didn't follow the instructions they'd been given, to their own cost. Children might even like to invent an example themselves of a time when they couldn't resist doing something they had been told not to, and the consequences of that.

Other comments on presentation: I have often found 'an empty box' to be a useful tool for drama. The box found in the middle of the road can result in lots of improvisation and role-play: Who does it belong to? What is it doing there? What is inside it? It need not be a superhero suit. There are lots of possibilities for assembly and drama lessons based on what an empty box might contain.

A set of keys is another basic yet rich prop. What does each key open? What is behind the door? Who left the keys there?

Promise you won't look

There is a large box lying in the middle of the stage with a ribbon around it. A young child enters with his or her father and points to the box

Child	Look Daddy! Birthday, birthday!
Dad	No. It's not your birthday yet. You've only just had your birthday.
Child	No, no. Birthday for me. Look!
Dad	*(notices the box)* No, it's not yours. You've had your presents. I wonder who it does belong to though. Very strange place to leave a present. *(looks around to see if there is anyone around, then goes up to the present and reads the label out loud)* Please do not open this box. Top secret.
Child	Open! Open! Box! Box!
Dad	No, I can't open it. It doesn't belong to us. Someone must have left it here and will come back later.
Child	Who? Baby? Mummy?
Dad	I don't know who. Now come on, or we'll be late for the bus.
Child	Look open!
Dad	Now I've told you. It's not ours.
Child	No. Box open. *(breaks away from Dad, runs to the box and pulls up the lid; stands with mouth open, staring)*
Dad	Now I've told you to leave it alone. *(obviously can't resist and approaches himself)* But seeing as it's open already, it won't do any harm to have a peek *(moves closer still to the box and looks in)*
Superhero	*(runs on from the side and grabs the box, pulling out the contents of cape, etc)* Hey! What are you doing with my outfit? You just couldn't stop yourself taking a look, could you? Now you've gone and spoiled it. Everybody will know that I'm Superman. What a spoilsport!
Dad	I'm ever so sorry. If I'd realised . . .
Child	*(leads Dad off, shaking head)* Naughty Daddy, naughty Daddy.

Superhero moves the box and places an apple there instead; enter boy and girl

Adam	Oh Eve, look at the lovely juicy apple. I'm starving. It's ages since we had breakfast.
Eve	What's this? *(sees there is a label attached to the apple and reads aloud)* Do not eat this apple or else. Or else what, I wonder?
Adam	Let's have a look. *(examines label)* Oh, I don't like the sound of that. Let's leave it where it is.
Eve	I thought you said you were hungry.
Adam	I'm not that hungry, and who knows who that apple belongs to and what will happen if we eat it?
Eve	Oh, come on! Don't be such a coward. 'Or else' probably just means that if we eat it we'll be cleverer than everybody else, or be able to do magic tricks or something. It doesn't say anything horrible's going to happen, does it?
Adam	Well no, not exactly . . . but . . .
Eve	Well then. If I can do it *(takes a bite)* so can you. *(passes it to Adam who also takes a bite)*
God	*(jumps onto the stage)* You've done it now.

Adam & Eve	*(jump in shock)* What do you mean, God?
God	You've done it now. You've only gone and eaten an apple from the tree of knowledge. You just couldn't resist it, could you?
Adam	We didn't mean to . . .
God	Didn't you read the label?
Eve	Well yes, but I just thought it was a trick to stop us from eating a lovely, juicy apple. Now, if you'd signed it …
God	Well, it's too late now.
Eve	What do you mean, too late?
God	I mean that that's the end of your life of luxury. No more spending your days counting the animals. From now on, you go to work and you can start off by digging up some weeds *(hands Adam a spade and exits)*
Adam & Eve	*(Look at each other)* That's another fine mess you've got me into. *(exit)*

Bluebeard's wife enters and speaks to the audience

Mrs B	My husband, Bluebeard, has gone away. He's gone away for a very long time. A very long time indeed. He's told me I can go anywhere in this house, except in that room. *(points to a door)* Now, I've been in all the other rooms and I'm bored. Perhaps the secret room is full of gold and jewels that he doesn't want me to know about. Perhaps it's full of the finest dresses. Perhaps it's the best room in the whole house and he just wants to save it for himself. *(she directs her questions at the audience)* What should I do? Should I go in or stay out? I don't know. I'll have to think about it. *(exits from the stage)*
Bluebeard	*(enters)* I've told my wife she's never to enter that room. *(points at the door)* She can go everywhere in this house, but behind that door. Oh dear, oh dear. I wonder if she'll end up like my other wives. There was Pamela and Sophie, Jane and Belinda, Karen and Freda, and Helen and Pat. Where are they now? I can see you're wondering. They're all in there. *(points at the room)* What's left of them. Ha, ha! *(exits from the stage and goes behind the secret door)*
Mrs B	*(reappears)* That's it. I've decided. I am his wife, after all. We should share everything. I'm going to see what's behind that door while my husband is out of the way. *(sneaks up to the door, tentatively starts to open it, Bluebeard jumps out)*
Bluebeard	Gotcha! *(chases his wife out of the hall or off the stage with a cardboard weapon; offstage there are shouts and groans, then his wife re-enters, wiping the weapon with a handkerchief)*
Mrs B	What a shame about Pamela and Sophie and the others. A good job I learned karate though. *(she puts down a cake on the stage and exits)*

Enter the Large family

Mrs Large	Now, remember everybody, we agreed. We'll leave this cake of Grandma's until we've all lost weight.
Baby Large	Do we have to? It looks so yummy.
Mrs Large	Yes we do. Now you can't be hungry after that delicious carrot soup, can you?

Baby Large	But I'm starving, Mummy.
Mrs Large	Don't be silly. How can you be starving? Now off you go to bed and don't forget to clean your teeth.

Baby Large exits, shuffling his or her feet in a strop

Miss Large	Don't worry, Mummy. I won't touch it. That watercress sandwich has filled me up. I couldn't eat another thing. Good night.
Mr Large	And I suppose it's time for my evening jog.
Mrs Large	It certainly is. I'll have a nice cup of hot water waiting for you when you get back.

Mr Large exits reluctantly

Mrs Large	Now they've all gone, it really would be rather rude if no one tries just a little of Granny's cake. Just a slice won't make any difference. *(sits down, cuts a slice, and is just about to take a bite when Miss Large returns)*
Miss Large	Mum! You cheat! Can I have some?
Mrs Large	Go on then, but just a sliver. We don't want to be greedy now, do we?

Just as they are eating, Baby Large comes on with his blanket

Baby Large	Ooh, naughty Mummy. I thought you said . . .
Mrs Large	All right, all right. You can have some too. But don't tell your dad.
Mr Large	*(enters)* Don't tell your dad what? So that's what you're up to? Come on then. Pass the knife.
Large family	Delicious!

Bibliography

Teachers may find the following books helpful:

Jack Zipes, *Creative Storytelling*, 1997, Routledge
Betty Rosen, *And None of it Was Nonsense*, 1988, Scholastic and Mary Glasgow Publications
Colin McNaughton, *Boo*, 1997, Picture Lions, Great Britain
Pat Hutchins, *Rosie's Walk*, 1998, Bodley Head Children's Books
Janet Stevens, *Tops and Bottoms*,1997, Hazar Publishing

Also available from Questions . . .

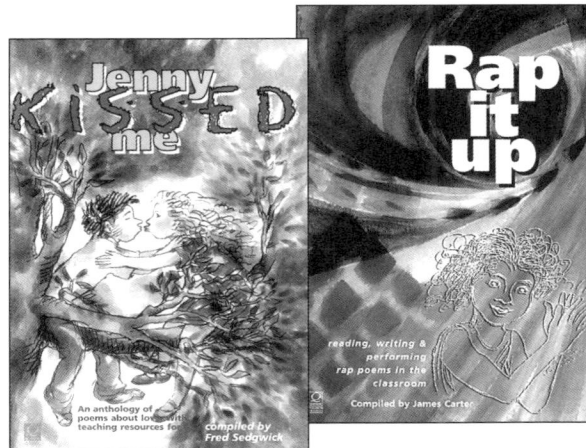

Jenny Kissed Me
by Fred Sedgwick

Jenny Kissed Me is an illustrated anthology of poems for Key Stage 2 that promotes an enjoyment of poetry and shows how children can learn to appreciate verse in a number of forms. This essential resource moves beyond the confines of the Literacy Hour and encourages children to incorporate their experiences into producing poetry of their own.

The teachers' notes include advice on dealing with each theme and ways of facilitating discussion, plus suggestions for follow-up work.

The book also offers:

- ideal opportunities for guided, group and independent reading;
- a thorough coverage of the National Literary Strategy's requirements;
- suggestions for motivating ways of studying poems, at text, sentence and word level.

ISBN: 1-84190-036-2
Price: £12.99

Rap It Up
by James Carter

This exciting and innovative anthology of rap poems for KS2 and KS3 teachers can be used both within and outside of the Literacy Hour. Featuring rap poems by popular and contemporary children's poets, the resource includes a CD featuring the poets Valerie Bloom and Brian Moses performing their own rap poems. It also contains three musical backing tracks for children to use in their own performances or to set their own poems to.

The teachers' notes include advice, ideas of reading, writing and performing raps, photocopiable activity sheets and suggestions for workshops. They also suggest appropriate context and opportunities in which children can:

- use rap poems by professional poets;
- explore both the form and content of rap poetry;
- practise aspects of creative writing, including brainstorming, improvising and re-drafting;
- explore rhyme, rhythm, narrative, narration, alliteration and assonance;
- create synonyms in words and phrases;
- develop performance and accompaniment skills.

ISBN: 1-84190-043-5
Price: £15.99

If you would like to place an order for these publications or would like to receive more information on the full range of products available from Questions Publishing Limited you can phone us on 0121 212 0919 or fax us on 0121 212 0959 or write to us at: The Questions Publishing Company Limited, Customer Services, 27 Frederick Street, Birmingham B1 3HH

Also available from Questions . . .

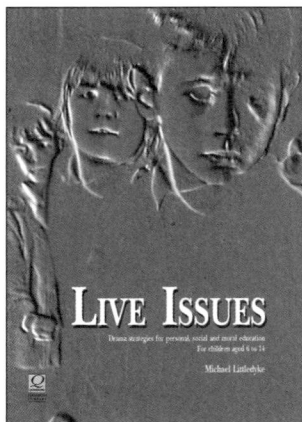

Live Issues
by Michael Littledyke

Live Issues is a collection of drama strategies for personal, social and moral education for children aged 6-14 years. Personal, social and moral themes, including 'Fairness', 'Social Choices', 'Discrimination', 'Sexual responsibility', religion, morality and environmental issues, are explored through more than 30 imaginative and stimulating drama structures.

The structures are summaries of drama sessions which the author has carried out with a wide age range and in many different contexts. They range from simple role-plays developed from family life, to elaborate dramas that can encompass the building of whole new worlds and bring in cross-curricular themes which can engage children for many weeks.

A complete resource, Live Issues provides teachers – even those with little or no experience in drama – with the means to use drama in a range of different settings. As well as the drama structures themselves, the book includes sections on:

- approaches to teaching morality
- techniques for teaching drama
- drama in the National Curriculum, including many suggestions for cross-curricular activities.

ISBN: 1-898149-51-8
Price: £19.99

If you would like to place an order for these publications or would like to receive more information on the full range of products available from Questions Publishing Limited you can phone us on 0121 212 0919 or fax us on 0121 212 0959 or write to us at: The Questions Publishing Company Limited, Customer Services, 27 Frederick Street, Birmingham B1 3HH